MW01641650

Max Cossack

WHITE MONEY

ISBN: 979-8-9879368-8-7

Previous books by Max Cossack in *The Wilder Bunch* series, in chronological order:

Khaybar, Minnesota (2018)
Zarah's Fire (2019)
Simple Grifts: A Comedy of Social Justice (2019)
Low Tech Killers (2020)
Where There Is No Man (2021)
Social Credit: A Comic Novel of Globalist Proportions (2021)
Blessed With All This Life (2022)
Naima's Fire (A Novelette) (2023)
Domesticated Terrorists (2023)
High Jingo (2024)

Other books published by VWAM include these by Susan Vass:

Ammo Grrrll Hits The Target (Volume 1)
Ammo Grrrll Aims True (Volume 2)
Ammo Grrrll Returns Fire (Volume 3)
Ammo Grrrll Is Home On The Range (Volume 4)
Ammo Grrrll Is A Straight Shooter (Volume 5)
Ammo Grrrll Reloads (Volume 6)
Ammo Grrrll Gets (a) Shot (Volume 7)
Double Tap: The Greatest Hits of Years 8 and 9 (Volume 8)
Over My Limit (Volume 9)

1 Morris Goldwater

As Goldwater lay in his makeshift bed in the stall, the sharp straw kept cutting into the tender flesh of his ear. He kept brushing it away and it kept springing back to poke him again.

He tugged his coat up toward his neck in another futile effort to warm himself.

“I’m afraid you’ll have to clear out.” A man’s gentle voice. “This is a horse barn, not a hobo camp.”

Goldwater looked up. A man stood over him. Down by his right leg the man held a sickle with a two-foot curved blade. Its metal shone in the dim light.

Goldwater had brought along his old five-shot 1849 Colt Pocket revolver. He left it in his coat pocket. He was just another unemployed stranger wandering a country overrun with vagrants and vagabonds since the Panic. To shoot a local his first night in town was to climb aboard the Hangman’s Express.

Besides, the man wasn’t really threatening Goldwater’s life. Likely he had grabbed up his farm tool just in case. It was a natural choice for a property owner when confronting a ragged stranger holed up in his barn.

Plus, as man in possession, his evictor commanded a moral advantage which Goldwater’s faith in property rights bound him to respect. It was the way of things.

So Goldwater didn’t argue. He grabbed his haversack and hoisted himself to his feet. He slung the haversack over one shoulder and walked toward the barn door. The man followed close behind, stern and sorrowful as a preacher forced by sad circumstance to call out one of his sinful flock.

The scent of the hostler's tobacco habit traveled with him. Goldwater had lost his fixings to the wind on that flatcar in Dakota Territory. The delectable tobacco fragrance reminded Goldwater how much he missed his pipe and his smokes.

The first step Goldwater took through the barn door, the bitter outside air smacked him in the eyes. He had taken refuge in this barn in the first place to avoid the outdoor hobo camp he had spotted near the tracks on his way into town. He paused and turned half-way and said, "Sir, my name is Morris Goldwater. May I inquire as to yours?"

"Victor Sadler" was the grunted answer. The man still held his sickle handy, down by his side, loose in his hand, just in case.

"Mr. Sadler," Goldwater began, "As you no doubt infer, at this moment I find myself in impecunious circumstance. Although I do reasonably expect that I will rectify this unfortunate condition in a day or two, I find myself unable at this moment to summon the price of hotel lodgings. I recognize that you do not want me sleeping in your stable. Would you allow me to assume some vacant spot out here in your corral? It seems devoid of stock."

A hint of sympathy flickered in Sadler's eyes. Sadler grunted assent and waved his sickle toward a corner just inside the corral fence.

Goldwater walked to the spot and probed it with his boot toe for horse turds. Not too bad—only a few petrified chips. Business at this stable must be bad. The Panic, probably. Like every other business. Goldwater nudged the few nuggets away with his boot until he had tidied up a turd-free space for himself.

Goldwater glanced back toward Sadler. The man had disappeared.

Goldwater settled himself onto the ground. He considered using his wool coat as a pillow, but he would make better use of it warming his body. He laid his haversack next to him. Too many years outdoors had proven the haversack too stiff and lumpy to make for a good pillow.

He wriggled around on his side until he found a low body-length gully which seemed to roughly fit his body shape. He folded his soft slouch hat into a wedge shape and positioned it on the ground for a pillow. He laid his head on top of it.

It had been days since Goldwater enjoyed even this much comfort. He closed his eyes and allowed sleep to sweep over his mind like a dark storm over the desert.

He was dreaming a dream of sweet Rosalie when an explosive thunderclap woke him up. He lifted his head straight into a torrent which flooded his eyes and flowed down his head and neck. He tried to stand but slipped. His body-shaped gully had turned into a slick mud hole.

Lightning flashed and for an instant lit the black sky and the barn and all the tiny town of Olam.

Goldwater stood and ran toward the barn door. The mud grabbed and sucked at his boots. Each step was heavier than the previous. The deluge surrounded him; he couldn't outrun it. Rain poured down on his head and body.

Goldwater plowed through the flood to the barn door and cracked it open just enough to slip through it sideways.

He swung the heavy door shut behind him. Safe from the storm for now, but soaked, he glanced around. Indoors again. But it was lightless as midnight in a coal bin.

Sadler had taken his tobacco incense and himself elsewhere. Goldwater didn't know where Sadler was spending the night, but it was not here. He didn't blame Sadler. A man took the best rest he could find wherever he could find it.

Goldwater fumbled a dry wood match out of the paraffin-covered bundle he kept in his left coat pocket and struck it with his thumbnail. A kerosene lantern hung nearby on a hook on the wall. He took the lantern down and used the last flicker of his match to light its wick. He carried the lantern in front of him farther into the barn.

An old saddle lay on the ground. Two worn saddle blankets lay across it. He lifted the blankets to his nose to test. He had smelled worse. At least they were dry.

A few horses shuffled and snuffled in their stalls nearby.

Goldwater found another empty stall with a thick pile of straw in it. The stall gate was open. He turned the lantern down to a low glow and bent and set it on the floor outside the stall and the combustible straw. No point in doing a Mrs. Leary.

He pushed the straw around with his boot to check for turds again. None. He crouched and scooped the thick straw into the shape of a mattress. He laid one blanket on top of the straw for a dry surface to lie on. He folded his hat and laid down and used it again for a pillow, this time soaked through. He stretched the second blanket over himself.

Like every other barn Goldwater had slept in, this one was unheated. Soaked as Goldwater was, the chill penetrated more than ever.

He wriggled his single skimpy saddle blanket up past his ears and wound it tight around his head. But the square-shaped blanket was too short: when he brought one end up to cover his neck, he exposed his wet calves and ankles, and when he pulled it down to wrap his feet and warm them, the other end of the blanket came only up to his navel and left his soaking shoulders and head and neck exposed.

This was his life now, tough choices from hard discomforts.

Southwest Arizona was supposed to be scorching hot. He supposed that in the summer it was hot enough. But this was winter, a winter not so frigid as Minnesota's, but cold enough to set Goldwater shivering until his jaw clenched and his neck ached.

The shivering was a wolf tearing him apart in its jaws, but he welcomed it. He had learned back in Minnesota that shivering warms you, in fact, can sometimes keep you alive, in a blizzard, for example. He'd seen a lot of those in the years he'd lived back in that other variety of Hell, the frigid version he'd read about in Dante long ago in that childhood school on the other side of the world.

Goldwater drew in a deep breath, deep as he could manage, and held it for a long moment. Life on the road had taught him that the sooner and more deeply he inhaled and accustomed himself to a stink, the less likely the stink would be to sicken him in the long run.

He let out the captured air and returned to his regular breathing.

Somewhere in the darkness, a horse shuffled its hooves and snuffled and snorted.

The horse snorted again, and then right away twice more. Or was it two different horses? Could a man distinguish horses by their snorts the way a man could distinguish men by their voices?

Goldwater could not.

But now came actual men's voices, low and angry. Maybe twenty feet or so distant, on the other side of the barn from the barn door Goldwater had slipped through. Must have come in through some other entrance.

One voice was Sadler's. "Goddammit, Doyle, you think you can threaten me?"

A man who must be Doyle answered, "Yes, by God, I do think so and I will, as I please!"

Another man threw in, "Don't push your luck, Sadler."

Two against one, it seemed.

Sadler said, "I got a right to my own claim, Roker."

Doyle said, "It won't be yours for long nohow. So why not sell while you can?"

"You think it's just me you need to drive out?" Sadler asked. "There's others."

"We'll take care of you right now," Roker said, "And get to the others later."

"The Hell you will," Sadler said. "If—"

A thud cut Sadler off. He grunted.

The grunt was followed by more thuds and grunts. one after another.

Goldwater knew the sound of a beating. He'd heard it often enough and seen it plenty too. Whoever they were, these Doyle and Roker characters were working Sadler over.

Were the two going to kill Sadler?

Should Goldwater butt in? After all, Sadler had relented and allowed Goldwater to sleep on his property.

Grudgingly, and only outside in the corral, of course, but still.

With every thud and groan the beating sounded worse. Goldwater pictured fist on head or belly. He thought he recognized the thump of wood hitting Sadler's body. A club, for sure.

Goldwater had to remember who he was and where he was. A wanderer far from home, in Arizona, which wasn't even a state, just a U.S. territory, and like any territory, notorious for lack of law or any other protection for the innocent or consequence to the guilty.

But still.

Goldwater reached across the floor and turned up his lantern. He grabbed it up by its handle and stood and stepped toward the men.

One man had pinioned Sadler's arms against the wall and above his head. The other held an axe handle cocked and drawn back, poised to pound into Sadler's skull. Fear and rage contorted Sadler's face as he struggled to break free.

The man with the axe handle was bleeding from a cut below his eye. Looked like Sadler had landed at least one good one.

"Hey!" Goldwater shouted, for lack of anything better.

All three men turned to look at Goldwater. Sadler wore a look of surprise, something like, "What are you doing here?", mingled with maybe a trace of hope.

The man with the axe handle took a single step toward Goldwater and said in Roker's voice, "Get lost, bum!"

"You mistake me, sir," Goldwater said. "I am not a bum."

"No, I got you pegged," Roker said. "You're a bum all right." He sneered Goldwater up and down. He caressed his club with affection. Goldwater was its next target.

"You are quite mistaken, sir," Goldwater said. "Despite my disheveled appearance, I am not a bum. I am rather a decent, hard-working man who came here in search of gainful employment. Bums do not work. I do."

Roker grunted. "I call that fancy language for a man what hides in a barn."

"Your language is as reprehensible as your behavior," Goldwater said. "I am not a man *what* hides in a barn, I am a man *who* hides in a barn."

At that, Doyle let go of Sadler's arms and stepped away and faced Goldwater. But his partner Doyle seemed to be smirking, at what, Goldwater wasn't sure.

On the other hand, Roker found nothing funny. He was still running his free hand up and down his club.

"Now, now," Goldwater told them. Goldwater had drawn his little Colt pocket revolver. He waved it now, from Roker to Doyle and back to Roker. He was relieved to see his own hand holding steady.

Even in the dim light cast by his lantern, Goldwater couldn't help noticing the sheer size of Doyle. The man seemed big as a bear, maybe even the grizzly variety. But for now at least, Doyle kept his smirk going, as if he were enjoying a theater show.

Goldwater had never actually shot anyone with his antique cap-and-ball pistol, not even in the desperation of Gettysburg, where he'd relied mainly on musket and then bayonet and when all else had failed, the musket's butt. He wasn't even sure his pistol load was in working order. He realized that he had not checked it since he left Minnesota, and he and his pistol and his powder had battled a lot of wet weather since then.

If either Doyle or Roker drew, Goldwater was dead.

But Doyle's smirk grew into an outright grin, and for whatever reason, Roker took Goldwater's bluff at face value. Maybe he also feared bee stings or horse fly bites. Under the unwavering aim of Goldwater's pistol barrel, the two men left Sadler leaning against his wall and let Goldwater herd them out of the barn.

Doyle grinned the whole way but said nothing. As Goldwater shut the barn door behind them, Roker turned and said, "Later, bum."

No point in responding. Goldwater found a spare plank on the ground and barred the door and walked back to Sadler. Sadler was leaning back against the wall to hold himself up. His legs looked soft as soggy straw.

Goldwater asked, "Are you okay?"

Sadler pushed himself away from the wall. He teetered for a moment, then straightened. He lifted his left hand and touched his bleeding lip. "I think I will be fine in a few minutes," he said. "Thanks to you."

He paused a moment, then added, "I now regret having rousted you."

"You had every right to bounce me," Goldwater said. "It is I who must apologize for ignoring you and resuming my trespass in your barn. The deluge churned the corral dirt into a bed of muddy inconvenience."

"Don't think a thing about it," Sadler said. He rubbed his torso as if checking for broken ribs. "I'm glad you ignored me."

Sadler straightened and took a deep breath. He seemed satisfied with the condition of his midsection. He regarded Goldwater for a long moment. "Say, Mr. Goldwater," he said, "You have an interesting manner of speech."

"I suppose," Goldwater admitted. "Many have so stated. Although I may have been pouring on the fancy talk with your attackers."

"Why do so?"

"Their incivility annoyed."

Sadler asked, "But you are educated?"

"Some," Goldwater said. "But, given my mode of dress, I was trying to present as respectable. Trying too hard, I suppose."

"You had me convinced," Sadler said. "And your fancy talk suggests you can spout those twenty-dollar words at will."

Goldwater shrugged a modest shrug.

"And did I hear you say you are willing to work?" Sadler asked.

"Yes," Goldwater said. "Eager, in fact."

"Then come with me," Sadler said. "I have just the job for you."

2 Marie Sadler

Goldwater picked up his haversack and slung it over his left shoulder. He followed Victor Sadler out of the barn and through the mud.

The rain had slowed to a mild drizzle. Only occasional fat drops hit Goldwater's bare cheek and neck. He gave up wearing his soggy hat and carried it in his left hand.

As they trekked toward wherever Sadler was taking them, Goldwater kept his right hand in his coat pocket and his eyes open for Doyle and Roker, who stayed out of sight.

After about fifty yards, Goldwater joined Sadler and climbed three short wooden steps onto a rickety boardwalk protected by an overhanging wood roof. They stopped for a moment to scrape the mud off their boot soles and heels against the edge of the walk. On their way, Sadler had picked up a thin slat of leftover lumber. He used it now to scrape the sides of his boots, then handed it to Goldwater to do the same.

Having cleaned their boots off at least some, the two clomped on without speaking for a block down the boardwalk. Sadler stopped at the front of a wood-frame building with a big sign hung high on its front. Goldwater craned his neck to read the sign. It said "Olam *Blade*."

A jumble of bullet holes in various diameters perforated the sign. Goldwater recognized the larger holes as .44 caliber. There was also a fair quantity of obvious shotgun pellet punctures. Sprinkled in among the others were a few bullet holes he could not classify.

Perhaps Sadler had collected more enemies than the two Goldwater had already met.

Above the front doorknob, someone had nailed plywood boards over what had once been a window. Sadler took a small brass key from the watch pocket of his trousers and inserted it into the keyhole to unlock the door. He grabbed the knob and swung the door out. He said, "Follow, please," and stepped through the doorway.

Goldwater followed Sadler. The instant they both stood in the entryway, Sadler slammed the door behind them and smacked a deadbolt shut. He turned and called into the next room, "Marie, it's me. I've brought a friend."

Marie came in from the other room. She was trim and sturdy and straight. She carried little flesh to spare. Goldwater read her as the kind of woman who had worked like a mule her entire life.

Marie had coiled her thick brown hair into a dark bun tightly wound behind her head. Her corset looked solid and stiff beneath. Over it she wore a floor-length dress of dark brown. She had tied on her front a canvas apron of bright white. In her arms she cradled a shotgun of steel gray.

She was pointing her shotgun off to her left side, but her posture announced her readiness to bring it to bear in an instant.

Sadler said, "Marie, this is my new friend—" he paused and turned.

"Morris Goldwater." Goldwater lifted his hat and set it on top of his head. The water dripped down his forehead into his eyes. He took off the soaked and misshapen thing and tipped it. It flopped over the fingers of his right hand.

She curtsied back a small curtsy, but a small smile played on her lips. He read her expression as skeptical.

Sadler said, "You should have seen him, Marie."

Marie said, “Victor, what happened to your face? In fact, what happened to the rest of you?”

“I had a little trouble with Doyle and his pet ruffian Roker,” Sadler said. He waved his hand toward Goldwater. “But this gentleman appeared out of nowhere like a miracle and faced them both down with his pistol. I owe him. He needs a dry place to sleep. And a job.”

Marie measured Goldwater with her glance. She seemed unimpressed.

“Please do not judge me by my disarray,” Goldwater told her. “I am not a bum.”

“Glad to hear it,” she said. “I admit I was wondering.” But her small hint of a smile broadened.

“I have recently made a hard journey,” Goldwater added. “And I am naturally not at my best. I can and will clean up.”

“You’ll have to clean up,” Sadler told Goldwater. “If you’re going to work as our editor.”

Sadler nodded towards the mechanism in the corner. For the first time, Goldwater noticed the small printing press there.

Goldwater asked, “Is that the job you have for me? Editing a newspaper?”

“Exactly,” Sadler said. “I am certain you have the gift.”

“But I have never written for a newspaper in my life,” Goldwater said. “Much less edited one.”

“Now’s your chance,” Sadler said. “And you told me you’re willing to work.”

“What makes you think I can do this thing?” Goldwater asked.

“Your manner of speech,” Sadler said. “Very elegant. Almost ceremonial, I might say. Besides, there can be no one else. You are it.”

Goldwater remained aware that Marie was watching him, probably judging him that way women so often judged men. In her manner she continued to remind him of Rosalie back home, assessing any stranger for his faults, open or hidden.

Goldwater waved one hand toward the press. “I know nothing about operating that machine.”

“I do,” Marie said. “You write and edit, and I’ll set whatever you write into type. That is the only hard part. Once the type is set, running the press is easy.”

Goldwater asked the obvious question. “You have a newspaper. Don’t you already have an editor?”

“We did,” Marie replied.

Two children came in through the same door Marie had used. The thin boy looked about nine, the girl maybe four or five. The girl hid behind Marie and peeked around her wide skirt. She hugged a small blanket in her left hand and sucked the thumb of her right.

The thin boy just stood and glared.

For a moment, no one said anything.

Sadler broke the silence. He said, “I’m hungry as a mongrel. Let’s eat first and talk it over.”

Sadler’s word “eat” reminded Goldwater that he had not tasted so much as a morsel in what—36 hours? Or was it 46? And what had he tasted? A brown chunk off an ancient apple handed him by some kind fellow traveler in that boxcar? The memory thrust the taste of the sour thing onto his tongue, rancid and bitter. He wobbled.

Marie shouted, “Victor!” and leapt forward. Victor joined her and together they grabbed Goldwater’s shoulders and braced him upright.

"I am fine," Goldwater told them. "I just need a minute. I can stand on my own. Please let me do so."

Marie let go and stepped away. Victor did not. Marie glared at Victor. "Didn't you ask your guest if he is hungry?"

Victor's response was a shrug and a helpless expression, very like the apologetic look Goldwater himself had offered Rosalie too many times to count.

Marie said, "Let us stuff our new editor with some victuals."

She led the others into the room she and the children had come from. In its middle stood a long rectangular table which took up almost the entire space, with six chairs around it. Victor guided Goldwater to one of the side chairs.

Goldwater sat. After the night's cold and soggy beginnings, resting his rear end on a chair at a table in the warm and dry indoors seemed a miracle. This promised to be a real set-down like his meals back in the coziness of his Minnesota home.

Twenty minutes later, Goldwater was digging in like a hobo at the mission. For the next little while, he did not bother to speak; all he did was chew and swallow. He cautioned himself not to wolf the huge portions Marie and Victor kept setting in front of him: mugs of strong black coffee, chunks of thick bread, two slabs of beef leaner and juicier than any he'd eaten since Ojibwa City, mounds of fried potatoes, and at least half a dozen soft-boiled eggs.

It was obvious his hosts were softening him up. But no way could Goldwater turn down this meal. He would blow out now and argue later.

At some point, after Victor had eaten his fill, Victor just watched, smiling a kind and generous smile which seemed to reflect a kind and generous soul within. At first Marie sat at the table as well, but she kept having to get up for more beef and potatoes and eggs, so finally she just stood and watched and waited for Victor to hand her the next empty plate to load.

The two kids stood silent, the girl indelibly sad and the boy relentlessly hostile.

Goldwater finished his feast with a huge slice of the proverbial American apple pie, as delectable as any pie a traveling man ever spotted cooling on a windowsill.

It wasn't just the food which satisfied. These people were sincere in their kindness and generosity. He already felt indebted.

Finally, Goldwater leaned back in his chair. He smiled first at Victor, then at Marie, then at the two kids.

He was about to speak when the boy said his first words since Goldwater had arrived: "You didn't wash up before eating."

Marie snapped out, "Roland! That is no fashion in which we speak to a guest!"

Roland answered, "You always make me wash up before eating." His was a grim and resolute plea for justice.

Goldwater had yet to see Roland smile.

Marie told Roland, "You can't expect a starving man to follow the same rules we follow, those of us who go about in the world like overstuffed steers fattening ourselves for market."

"That's right, Roland," Victor said. "Until you have walked in a man's shoes, you must not criticize him. It is rude."

Goldwater recalled how his own father and mother had teamed up to tyrannize him. "You are correct, Roland," Goldwater told the boy. "I apologize. It was disrespectful of me to sit down at this table without caring first for personal hygiene. If you will direct me to a wash basin where I can clean myself off, I will take care of that now."

He smiled at Marie and said, “Even if only belatedly.”

Roland remained stone-faced. He muttered, “Well, come on, then.”

Without waiting for Goldwater, Roland turned and walked away. Goldwater stood and followed him into the kitchen and then into a small room off to its side. On a stand in the room sat a porcelain pitcher and bowl. Both were empty.

Without saying a word, Roland grabbed the pitcher. He carried it into the kitchen and outside through the kitchen door. A moment later, he came back, his hair sopping wet and his pitcher overflowing.

Goldwater asked, “Raining again?”

Roland nodded. He poured the pitcherful of water into the basin. He set the pitcher down on the stand and walked out of the room.

Goldwater took off his coat and hung it on a convenient hook on the wall. He rolled up his sleeves and washed his hands and face and dried off with the towel hanging on the rack.

Civilization, even in this desolate desert place. A home, nothing like a hobo camp or a railroad roundhouse. This new-model house even boasted indoor plumbing. Goldwater made use of it and then washed himself again. He picked up his coat and left the washroom and walked through the kitchen back to the family table.

Goldwater’s haversack lay on the floor where he must have dropped it. He did not recall doing that. He picked it up and set it on the empty chair next to him.

What now? Goldwater looked around. The entire family sat at the table, waiting on him. Victor was smiling. Marie seemed concerned about something or other. The little girl sat on

Marie's lap, still clutching her blanket and sucking her thumb. Roland still clenched his face tight.

Goldwater spoke first. "First of all, let me express to everyone here my gratitude. I have not enjoyed a meal like this in eons." He nodded and smiled around the table at each family member, including Roland.

Goldwater went on. "I know that I do not present the image of a gentleman, but I am, or I should say, have been, a solid citizen. I own and operate The Goldwater Emporium in Ojibwa City, Minnesota. It is or was a prosperous business I am proud to have built with my own hands. But we must all recognize that the Panic has imposed financial difficulties on our country, including on my business and on my entire hometown. These difficulties have forced me to travel here."

"All the way from Minnesota?" Marie asked.

"Yes," Goldwater replied. "You see, I made a great friend during the War, a fellow soldier. At a propitious moment, when I happened to be flush, I lent him a small sum. To be honest, I lent the money only from gratitude. I considered it a gift. But to my astonishment, he turned my gift into an investment which has paid off. I came to Olam to reap the reward. And that is why I cannot accept your generous offer to edit your newspaper. But I promise that as soon as I come into my investment, I will repay your generosity as many times over as you will allow."

Victor asked, "What did your friend invest in?"

"White money," Goldwater said.

"White money?" Marie asked,

"That is what we call silver," Goldwater said. "On the road."

"Then you came to the right town," Victor said. "Olam is full of rich silver mines. Which is your friend's?"

"The Bloody Angle," Goldwater said. "Do you know it?"

"I do," Victor said.

Marie asked, "Is your friend's name John Taff?"

"Why, yes," Goldwater said.

"Oh dear," Marie said.

Goldwater asked, "Why 'oh dear'?"

She frowned first at Victor then at Goldwater. "I am afraid Mr. Taff is dead."

3 John Taff

News of John Taff's death was another shock in the battalions of shocks which had shaken Goldwater in the past few years. He felt the same sinking in his belly he had felt when the Panic hit full force and he stood behind his counter and saw his Emporium desolate of paying customers.

"Of what did he die?" Goldwater asked.

"His mine collapsed on him," Victor said. "It is a common story. We live in a shoddyocracy. In this town, they construct too many mines too shabbily and in too much of a hurry."

"I see," Goldwater said, although he didn't. Shabby construction did not square with what he knew about John Taff. The man was a perfectionist.

Goldwater picked up and opened his haversack and dug out a folded letter. He handed it to Victor. "So what is this worth?"

Morris Goldwater

General Delivery

Ojibwa City, Minnesota

October 7

Dear Goldwater,

Well, old Cumradd,I have finally Strukk it, by which I

mean you have Strukk it with me, if you recall my Ooth I swore to you.

If not, I will remind you here. It was that time in the field hospitel right after Gettysburg when I sworr a solemn Ooth that you will share in any good fortune I ever encounter in my Life, so far pretty worthless, if you want one man's opinyan, in which I am Shure I am Not Alone.

I have worked more than ten years to make good on the Ooth I sworr. And now I can.

You see, I have made a Silver Strike in a town called Olam, Arizona. It is a very big Strike and I am confidant will support more than won man in luxury and wealth for the rest of his Naturel Life. I call my mine The Bloody Angle. I am sure you reconize the inspiration for the name.

I have properly registerred my Claim and also now the Trannsfer of haff-interest to you in your name. So it is all set up for you.

If you can manaj it, this will be a good time to cumme and see your diggings for yourselfe. I am kwite confidant you will be very satisfied with yure new mine The Bloody Angle.

Your Friend,

John Taff

Victor examined the letter for a moment. He said nothing. He passed it to Marie.

She read it, then asked Goldwater, "This letter brought you here?"

"Yes," Goldwater said. "The Panic has destroyed my business. No one in my town has any cash, especially since Congress passed that damnable Coinage Act and only gold is accounted hard money. Our people have gone back to barter, as if we all lived in olden times before money existed. My Emporium takes in more eggs than my wife and children can eat. The occasional complete chicken comes as a gift from heaven."

Marie nodded in sympathy. "Like so many all over our country."

Victor said, "So Mr. Taff's letter must have seemed a miracle."

Goldwater nodded. "True."

Victor asked, "What did you do for this Taff fellow that filled him with such gratitude?"

Goldwater slipped the question. Instead, he said, "I left most of our existing cash in my wife's capable hands to take care of herself and our children. Things did not go my way on the journey here. I had no money left over for lodging, which is the reason you found me in your barn."

"Lucky for me," Victor said.

Marie told Goldwater, "But you face obstacles, I fear, in winning your claim."

"My friend's claim is not so rich as he thought?"

"Oh, I think it must be," Marie said. "Likely not as rich as the Comstock or the Ophir, but rich enough. Many in Olam are."

"Your obstacle will come when you try to enforce your claim," Victor said. "All mining claims hereabouts are subject to court disputes."

"My letter will not do?" Goldwater asked.

Victor glanced at Marie. She said, "You will have to ask lawyer Lamont. He is young, but smart and devoted. He represents all the miners here in their claims against Doyle."

"Doyle?" Goldwater said to Victor. "The same man I chased off last night? The man who tamped you up?"

At their blank expressions, Goldwater explained, "I mean, beat you."

"Not just me," Victor said. "Many others as well. It is his way."

"His way to what?" Goldwater asked.

"To immense wealth," Victor said. "He has a simple plan; he takes. He hires toughs like Roker to help make the taking stick, and worse, he is tough enough himself."

"Is there no law here?" Goldwater asked.

"Sort of," Marie said. "But Doyle has Judge Cady in his pocket. You will see."

4 Mel The Barber

After dinner, the Sadlers avoided all Goldwater's questions about his chances for his claim. Lawyer Lamont would explain. And they said nothing more about their offer to edit the *Blade*.

When Victor filled and lit his pipe, Marie seemed to notice the look on Goldwater's face. She asked him, "Do you take a pipe?"

"I am afraid I do," Goldwater said. "It is a habit I cannot shake. But I lost my fixings on the journey here."

"Just a moment," she said. She stood and walked out of the room. A moment later, she returned with a pipe and handed it to Goldwater. "This was our brother's," she said. "And now it is yours."

Goldwater looked over the pipe. It was a fine briarwood, a long-stemmed beauty. He did not ask why her brother no longer needed it. There was always a reason, and the reason was always the same.

Victor waved an invitation toward the glass tobacco jar sitting at the end of the table. Goldwater accepted his invitation and loaded his new pipe and savored the first good smoke he had enjoyed in weeks. It was a fine tobacco, a mellow aromatic blending latakia and cavendish, with the addition of a small portion of burley and a pinch of bright Virginia.

The two men puffed away, and the three new friends sat and chatted until exhaustion caught up to Goldwater and he faded off in the middle of Victor's sentence.

Marie led Goldwater upstairs to a real bed. He took off his boots and fell onto the bed still wearing his clothes, which had already dried in the desert air.

It was an unheated bedroom on the third floor, far from the first-floor coal stove, but Marie dumped a pile of heavy wool blankets onto Goldwater and buried him under them. He slept in unaccustomed bliss through the night, toasty and dry.

When he awoke the next morning, he luxuriated in the warmth of his covers for a long time before he could force himself out of his comfort into the room's cold January air.

His hosts had furnished his room with a chamber pot and a full wash basin and towels. He performed some calisthenics to warm himself, then took off his road clothes and piled them in the corner. Naked, he used the chamber pot and used the wash basin to clean and dry his body from top to bottom.

Goldwater laid his haversack on his bed and opened it. With great care he unrolled and dressed himself in the clean underwear and the glad rags he had packed at home, his black wool trousers, his boiled white shirt with detachable collar, a candy-striped vest, and gray pinstripe suitcoat.

This was the second-best suit he had brought. The best he would save for a special occasion.

He looked over the red silk cravat he held in his hands. Should he put it on? He had bought it on impulse, in a mad moment long before the Panic, in a fancy St. Paul haberdashery.

He had never worn it. There was never an Ojibwa City occasion for any personal display this fancy.

He had packed it in anticipation of celebrating his mining claim. Now it seemed as out-of-place in Olam as it had been in Ojibwa City. He folded it with care and placed it back in his haversack.

He topped off his fancy attire with the derby hat he had blocked, wrapped, boxed and stored in the haversack for just this moment.

The room lacked a mirror, so he moved about and angled himself until he could see his reflection in the window. Very satisfying. Dapper once more. He strolled downstairs.

He carried the chamber pot with him through the kitchen and into the washroom and emptied and flushed it away in the toilet there.

He washed his hands and left the pot on the bathroom floor and walked back into the kitchen. Marie was putting together a breakfast almost as magnificent as his supper the night before.

While he fed himself eggs and grits and toast, she sipped coffee from a mug and kept him company. Victor was busy just now, out of the house since early morning. He operated several ventures, including not only the newspaper, which she reminded Goldwater they meant to reopen with his help, but also a small dry goods store and the stable where Goldwater had carried out his rescue.

Like John Taff's mining claim, the Sadler claim was tied up in Judge Cady's court.

Marie asked about Goldwater's family back home. He found himself rambling about his wife Rosalie and their four boys and two girls.

She nodded along. They chatted a while about her own life, which is how Goldwater learned that she and Victor were brother and sister and that Roland belonged to neither of them, but to a widower brother who had died in yet another mining accident.

Marie was a widow herself but not widow to a miner. "He was a railroad brakeman," was all Marie said and all she needed to say. "I'm lucky to have our little Charlotte still with me."

The brakeman's job was the most hazardous work Goldwater knew of. It was even more dangerous than mining.

Since each separate car relied on its own separate brakes, and the brakes were built into its car on the outside, a brakeman had to clamber along on the tops of moving trains, from car to car, winter and summer, in calm and rough weather, sunny or stormy.

Not to mention the risks brakemen faced from violent tramps and bums bent on riding the rails for free.

Goldwater had dodged a few brakemen in his own travels. Ironically, it seemed more considerate to change the subject from Marie's dead husband back to her dead brother. He said, "There seem to be a lot of mining accidents around here."

"Yes," she answered. "Mining is a dangerous job, especially if you go up against Doyle."

"Did your brother go up against Doyle?"

"No more than any other."

He asked, "By which you mean, no more than John Taff?"

Her face darkened, but she said nothing.

He asked, "Is there a laundry in town?"

She asked, "Do you have money for such?"

"Not really," he said.

"Didn't you bring any cash along on your journey here?"

"Robbed," One more misfortune.

"I will do your laundry," Marie said. "At least, for any part of those rags of yours worth saving. Please bring them downstairs."

When he objected, she waved him off, saying, "If you insist, I will charge you, but I will wait to take any payment out of your salary as editor when that time comes, which I am confident it will, assuming your mining claim does not pan out. Of course, if it does pan out, I need not concern myself, as you will then possess vastly more wealth than Victor and me."

He said, “Perhaps in the meantime, I can work off my board here by clerking for Victor in his store.”

“That would be fine,” she said. “Although the Panic has left its mark in Olam too. Because of the silver mines, things are not as desperate in our town as back east in yours, but among Doyle’s many operations, he also runs his own store in competition with ours, which leaves little business left over for Victor. I mean, Victor may not have any use for your help.”

At Goldwater’s disappointed expression, she added, “But it can hurt nothing to ask him.”

One phrase of hers struck Goldwater as strange. He asked, “By ‘back east’ I assume you mean Minnesota?”

“Of course,” she said.

“I must be getting old,” he said. “When I first moved to Minnesota as a boy not that many years ago, that was ‘The West’. Now it is ‘The East’.”

“Everything changes fast in this country,” she said. “It gets hard to keep our bearings.”

He asked, “Is there a barber shop in town? As you see, I could do with a shave and a haircut.”

She smiled. “Those I cannot help you with. But just mention our name to Mel the Barber and he will no doubt extend you credit.”

Goldwater thanked her and excused himself. He walked out through the front door onto the Boardwalk and into the cool winter sunshine.

As he walked, he thought about Marie. She was not what some would consider a beautiful woman, but she was warm and strong, and she displayed an awareness of herself as a physical being. It had something to do with the way she carried herself.

But surely she was not interested in Goldwater anyway. He vowed not to betray to her his awareness of her as a woman. That would be rude and embarrassing.

He followed Marie's directions a block down the boardwalk until he spotted the familiar red-and-white striped pole of a barbershop and went in.

The barber, who must be Mel, was shaving a man in his big barber chair. The face under the white lather was Roker's.

Goldwater froze where he stood, undecided. His first impulse was to turn around and walk out. But doing that might only draw unwelcome attention.

Thankfully, Roker's glance passed over him with uninterest. Roker must not recognize Goldwater in this morning's fine clothes. A blessing for sure.

Mel asked him, "Did you come for a shave and a haircut, sir?"

Goldwater only nodded. Why let Roker hear his voice?

"Please take a seat, sir," Mel said. "You're next, after my other customer." He gestured toward a man, sitting in the rightmost of the three chairs by the wall.

Doyle, naturally.

Doyle didn't look up. He seemed absorbed in his copy of the *National Police Gazette*, easy to recognize from its pink tabloid pages.

Goldwater took the leftmost chair, leaving one empty seat between Doyle and him. Another copy of the *Gazette* lay on the empty chair. Goldwater picked it up and opened it and lifted it high to cover his face.

Doyle took one glance at Goldwater and his *Gazette* and went back to his own paper. He showed no more interest in Goldwater than Roker had.

Goldwater sat stiff and clutched the *Gazette* high in front.

He might as well turn the pages and read. Its pages featured the usual engravings of buxom women in tights, lurid yarns detailing notorious murders, and chronicles celebrating the triumphs and disasters of boxers and baseballists.

Having grown up in Vienna, Goldwater knew little about the American ball game, although he enjoyed watching his sons go at it. In camp games during the War, to the amusement of his fellow soldiers, he had taken a few token swings himself. He failed to make contact even once. Like everything else, hitting a thrown ball with a stick was harder than it looked.

But he liked watching his sons play, and it came naturally to them, which gratified him, since he wanted them to be true Americans, and according to every authority, baseball was the official American game. Every town in Minnesota had its own ball team. The Dropo boys' baseballist skills made them famous throughout the state.

Boxing was a different matter. It was not a mere game, but practical, so Goldwater read the boxing stories with great care. The street and tavern fights he had witnessed in America were usually brutal clumsy affairs absent science or skill, frequently involving the chair or club or bottle nearest to hand.

He had never witnessed the kind of illegal professional fight described in the Gazette. In the professional fights he read of here, men fought according to what the *Gazette* called the "London Prize Ring Rules."

Goldwater ran across a full-page engraving of two men stripped to the waist, their clenched bare knuckles held upright before them, perhaps in order to prevent their opponents from grappling or grabbing their heads and necks. He tried to imagine for himself how he would use such a stance to avoid and deliver clinches and punches. Goldwater had never brawled in America or back in the old country.

The *Gazette* declared an Englishman named Mel Goss to be the American professional champion. He had once fought a bout which lasted 66 rounds spread over three hours.

Not as long as some military battles, but an impressive display of stamina nonetheless.

Engrossed in his reading, Goldwater almost forgot himself. At the thud of boots hitting the floor, he looked up from his paper.

Roker had got up from his chair. Mel was shaking out his barber's cape over the floor. Roker walked over to the door. He took up a bodyguard's station there and began to watch the street up and down.

Doyle stood to take his turn in the barber chair.

Goldwater raised his *Gazette* higher. If either of these two new enemies recognized him, he stood no chance.

That sobering thought brought Goldwater's attention to the pistol Roker wore holstered on his hip. As a merchant who sold guns of all kinds, Goldwater had no trouble recognizing it as a .44 caliber Colt Single Action Army Peacemaker, one of the most powerful handguns in the world, and standard issue for the U.S. Army.

One slug from a .44 would outperform several rounds from Goldwater's feeble .31-caliber percussion revolver.

Goldwater snuck his right hand under his coat and felt in his inside pocket. Nothing there. He must have left his pistol in his room back at the Sadler house.

Goldwater was sitting unarmed in a cramped space with two rough men he had just the night before threatened with his own gun, which he had now like an idiot managed to leave behind .

He mentally cursed himself and sent a silent message of regret to Rosalie and his children back home.

Goldwater laid his paper on his knees and stared at the floor. He used his peripheral vision to try to watch both enemies at the same time. He could not risk eye contact.

Mel the Barber spent what seemed a considerable time on Doyle's shave. When Mel finished, he wiped his customer's face off with a fresh hot towel. Doyle stood and took off the barber's cape and handed it to Mel with a single Gold Eagle. When Mel offered a few coins as change, Doyle shrugged him off with a magnanimous grin. He strode to the door.

In the bright Arizona sunlight streaming through the window, his size and obvious power intimidated even more than it had in Sadler's barn the night before.

Unlike Roker, he wore no gun on his hip. Goldwater guessed Doyle wore a shoulder holster rig under his suitcoat, as the most dangerous men often did. Or he carried in an inside pocket with slick fabric sewn in for an easy draw, like a few men even more dangerous.

Or maybe this colossus didn't need a gun to impose his will on any man.

Roker pushed the door open ahead of Doyle and stepped outside and held it for his boss. Doyle stepped to the door. He stopped in the doorway and turned and looked for the first time straight at Goldwater. He asked, "Did you bring your peashooter?"

Careful not to betray his fear with a shaky voice, Goldwater only shook his head.

Doyle said, "Next time, bring it." He turned and left. Roker followed him, but not before stepping back in and tossing Goldwater one goodbye sneer.

The flush heated Goldwater's neck and face. He stood and took the barber chair. He muttered to Mel, "The Sadlers sent me."

Mel gave a small smile of sympathy and nodded. "I guessed as much," he said. "Pay me when you can," and gave Goldwater his shave and haircut.

Neither said more.

5 Horses

Goldwater stepped through Mel's door onto the Boardwalk. Doyle and Roker had just mounted the horses they must have tied to a nearby hitching post.

To his relief, the two men had already turned to head up the street and didn't seem to notice him. They spurred their horses and rode away. Clumps of mud flew behind the hooves.

Why would anyone want a horse in this tiny town? A man could travel on foot from one end to the other in a half hour or less.

Goldwater feared and hated horses.

His fear started with a disaster Goldwater witnessed as a small child on the streets of Vienna.

This particular horse had seemed the ideal domesticated animal, tame and amiable and harmless as a puppy. He wore a cute straw hat with flowers on top. His big brown ears waved through two holes in his hat as if to signal his gentle nature. Passersby fed him apples. Once, as a tiny boy, urged by his mother, Goldwater himself had handed the horse a carrot and watched with satisfaction as the animal munched it down.

One day, for no reason, the horse bolted out of human control and turned in an instant into a monster of reckless destruction. Crazed by some unknown impulse, he stampeded through the streets, yanking his carriage and its hapless driver this way and that behind him. The carriage careened loose and crashed into the veranda in back of one of Vienna's famed coffee houses, killing a gentleman and a lady and injuring a dozen more customers.

From then on, Goldwater suspected even the mildest horse of plotting evil. A horse was a behemoth with a neck thick as a tree trunk, who glared out at the world from two rolling white eyes the size of cueballs, who bared giant teeth blazing with the sheen of cavalry sabers, and who displayed a terrifying inclination to kick to death anyone who wandered onto his wrong side, which, as far as Goldwater could tell, might be any side which the horse decided for random horse reasons to disapprove of.

And the animal's legs and hooves: powerful enough to kick any man or beast into oblivion. On a country road outside Ojibwa City one day, Goldwater had come across the carcass of a mountain lion with a crushed skull. The local farmer told Goldwater that the big cat had made the mistake of irritating a thoroughly domesticated horse.

Goldwater did not want to irritate a horse. In fact, he wanted nothing to do with any horse ever.

Every time Goldwater mentioned to Rosalie his suspicion that this or that horse was eyeballing him as if eager for the first chance to get him, Rosalie told him he was crazy.

Goldwater hid his aversion from his children, although he supposed his older ones had caught on by now. But they never said anything.

Of course, in a world where most people traveled by horse, avoiding them was a challenge. Goldwater congratulated himself on the fact that he did a pretty good job of staying away from these monsters.

One more reason to travel by train, even without a ticket.

.

6 Horatio Lamont

After Mel the Barber had performed his magic, Goldwater indulged his vanity with a once-over in Mel's hand-held mirror. What he saw satisfied.

With Doyle and Roker out of sight, and feeling like a new man, or at least the old man restored, Goldwater sauntered down the Boardwalk.

He was once again a solid citizen, the kind of man who could marry a fine woman and raise decent children and run a prosperous business. And maybe even operate a silver mine.

Another half-block down the Boardwalk, he spotted another building with boarded up windows. Above this one's door hung a sign reading "Law Office."

Goldwater knocked. Someone cracked the door open from inside about half an inch. All Goldwater saw was one eye and part of a nose. Feeling a little silly, Goldwater murmured, "The Sadlers sent me. I'm Goldwater."

"I'm lawyer Horatio Lamont," the man said. He opened the door another foot or two and stepped back to make room for Goldwater to slide in.

Goldwater slipped through the narrow opening.

Loose in his right hand, Lamont held a dragoon revolver, not quite the size of a field Howitzer.

Lamont wasted no time in locking the door behind Goldwater, who said, just to make sure he got the point across, "As I mentioned, I'm a friend of the Sadlers."

"Of course," Lamont said. "That's why you made it inside."

The two men shook hands.

It was a small office, only about fifteen-by-fifteen feet. The sole decoration was Lamont's law license hanging framed on the wall.

Lamont looked even younger than Marie had suggested—in his early twenties at the oldest. He wore a prim dark suit and a pinstripe shirt. His starched white collar encircled a thin neck. He had shaved his round cheeks pink. He parted his straight brown hair neat down the middle in a style Goldwater had never seen before. Must be the latest fashion back East. He smelled of a pleasant pomade Goldwater did not recognize.

Goldwater made a mental note to learn the brand. Maybe he should carry the pomade once he got his Emporium up and running again.

Lamont waved for Goldwater to sit on a simple stool in front of a desk which was nothing more than a plywood board laid across two sawhorses. Without another word, Lamont seated himself on the bare unfinished wood chair behind his mock desk and folded his hands.

Goldwater took John Taff's letter out of his inside coat pocket. He handed it to Lamont and waited for Lamont to read it. Lamont spent a long time on this short letter. From time to time, Lamont penciled a note or two on a yellow pad on his board. It was at least ten minutes before he handed the letter back to Goldwater. His diligence impressed.

Goldwater folded the letter and put it back in his inside coat pocket.

"Well," Lamont said. "Your letter presents some interesting issues."

"How so?" Goldwater asked. As a store owner, he was familiar with some commercial codes, but he knew little about mining law, assuming that mining law was what Lamont was talking about.

Lamont said, "For example, there's the legal issue as to whether the letter constitutes an effective and enforceable transfer of John Taff's interest in the mine."

"Does it?" Goldwater asked.

"That is difficult to say just yet."

Typical lawyer response. "Okay," Goldwater said. "What are the other issues?"

Lamont rubbed his smooth young chin. "Even if your claim is enforceable in law in general, there's also the obvious question whether you can actually enforce it in our local court system as it currently operates."

"I'm not sure I understand," Goldwater said. "The Sadlers mentioned something about that. That was one of the things they left vague."

"I do not blame them," Lamont said. "The reality can be vague as well."

"I do not understand," Goldwater admitted.

"The Sadlers didn't fill you in on the goings on?"

"No," Goldwater said. "They left that to you."

"So I will start with the situation overall," Lamont said. "Then we'll talk about your letter."

"Okay," Goldwater said. Lawyers liked to draw out their explanations.

Lamont said, "The situation overall is that Alexander Doyle wanted to corner all the silver in this part of Arizona Territory. But he was too smart to start local. He went direct to the power, which operates out of Washington, DC. After all, we're only a territory, not a state. Doyle set up a corporation he calls "Arizona Silver." but which most people around just call "The Silver Ring."

"The Silver Ring," Goldwater echoed. He rolled the phrase around in his mind. A few years earlier, two investors named Fisk and Gould had tried to corner all America's gold with their "Gold Ring." President Grant had foiled their scheme, but a near-Panic had followed the subsequent crash in the price of gold.

"The Silver Ring," Lamont repeated back. "When Doyle incorporated his Silver Ring, he allocated only 49% of stock to invest in mining. He allocated 51% for Washington politicians. He then spread this 51% around to key men. These powerful men convinced the President to appoint one of their own as federal judge for Arizona Territory. That's Doyle's man Judge Cady."

"Okay," Goldwater said.

"Then there's Doyle's lawyer Gentry Abbey. He'll run into Cady's Court with any excuse he can come up with and get Judge Cady to put any mine into Receivership. Do you know what a Receivership is?"

"Help me out, please," Goldwater said.

Lamont leaned forward. "If there's any doubt about a claim's ownership—and Judge Cady always finds doubt—then Cady appoints Doyle as Receiver of the mine. A Receiver's duty is to operate the mine for the benefit of the true owner, once the true owner can be determined. But Doyle mines the claim as fast as he can while the Court dawdles over the case. They stretch out the proceedings until all the silver ore is gone."

Goldwater knew enough to ask, "Doesn't a Receiver like Doyle have to post bond while he operates the mine?"

"Good question," Lamont said. "I'm glad to see you understand a little of the law. Doyle does have to post bond, but that amounts to nothing more than some puny amount like a thousand dollars a day."

"A thousand a day doesn't sound so puny."

"It is puny enough when they are digging five thousand a day out of the mine."

Goldwater nodded. "Clever, I suppose."

"That is not all," Lamont said. "The mine is like a pig in a slaughterhouse. They sell even the squeal. Doyle and his cronies are showing off the silver and the profits back East so they can print more stock certificates and sell more stock. They're making a fortune just from selling their watered stock. Once they use up the mine, they'll dump their corporation and take to the hills."

Goldwater asked one question more. "Where does the money go? I mean from operating the mines in the meantime? I mean, isn't the revenue being held in some special account for the Receivership?"

"Another good question," Lamont said. "They loot the mines with fake expenses. Meanwhile, the law slumbers, or at best slithers along like a slug on a leaf. By the time I get the mines restored to their rightful owners, the mines will be all played out. That will include your claim, of course."

"So what can I do?" Goldwater asked.

"We can make a record in Court," Lamont said. "If we get this mess straightened out in the end, maybe you'll wind up with something."

"You do not promise much," Goldwater said.

Lamont shrugged. "It's my duty to be honest with you."

Goldwater grinned. "And you are doing your duty with admirable thoroughness."

Lamont grinned back. "I take that as a compliment."

"You must know that I have no money to pay," Goldwater said.

"I figured as much," Lamont said. "But you will be helping me with my other clients, the few who can pay some. The more miners who fight, the better off every miner will be."

"You make it all sound pretty hopeless," Goldwater said. "Helpless and hopeless. Must I just wait things out?""

"No," Lamont said. "I am not waiting for anything or anyone. I am just saying the battle is yet to be fought to the end, although, for now, Doyle is winning, and by a lot."

"Which brings up something else you can do for me," Goldwater said.

"What more?" Lamont asked. "I have already promised I will go to court with you for free. And in court I am a warrior."

"My friend John Taff," Goldwater said. "What can you tell me about this mine cave-in that is supposed to have killed him?"

Lamont said, "What makes you ask?"

"Oh, nothing much," Goldwater said. "Other than the way the Sadlers dodged that question when I put it to them direct. And the other Sadler brother died from a cave-in too, did he not?"

Lamont leaned back and away from Goldwater. He said, "I do not claim to know the answer to questions like those."

He seemed to spot Goldwater's doubtful expression. He said, "I mean I really do not know."

Goldwater asked, "How would I find out?"

7 The War

As Goldwater made his way down the Boardwalk back to the Sadler House, his confusion and frustration solidified into anger.

Much of this anger he directed at himself. He had failed his best friend. After receiving John's letter, he could have bought a ticket and come to Olam right away. Maybe John would still be alive. But discouraged by his financial struggles, Goldwater had been too damned cheap.

True, Goldwater could point a finger at the damnable Panic, but he had to shoulder some portion of blame himself.

John Taff was not only Goldwater's comrade and best friend but a hero of the world at large. Taff was the bravest man Goldwater had ever known.

Goldwater never understood how Taff managed it, but he took every one of the many setbacks life imposed on him with a patient smile. This was an ability Goldwater admired but could never develop in himself.

Goldwater had lived out his childhood in Vienna and Taff grew up in Germany. When they met they shared the German language as their mother tongues and bonded quickly. Taff was older than Goldwater and already tested in war, which Goldwater was not. Taff became Goldwater's mentor as a soldier and as a man. Goldwater was sure he would not have survived the war without Taff watching out for him.

All Goldwater had given John Taff in return was one moment of madness when he threw himself between Taff and a Confederate bayonet.

In April 1861, immediately after the Confederates fired on Fort Sumter, Minnesota was the first state to offer troops to meet Lincoln's call for 75,000 Union volunteers. In May, Taff and Goldwater and the other volunteers boarded transport boats headed down the Mississippi River from Fort Snelling. After debarking at a downriver port, they rode trains east to Virginia. Only two months later, in July 1861, the Minnesota volunteers were among the minority of Union troops to acquit themselves well in the disastrous Union defeat at the first Battle of Bull Run.

Two years later, on July 2, 1863, the second day of the Battle of Gettysburg, twelve hundred Confederate soldiers were threatening to capture the critical Union stronghold on Cemetery Ridge when a general ordered the 250 men of the First Minnesota Regiment to charge into the Confederate attack. The Regiment suffered more than 80% casualties in the next five minutes, but their charge gave Union forces time to bring in reinforcements and save not only the day but ultimately the entire battle for the Union.

Although Taff was wounded, he and Goldwater were two survivors.

After the war, many discharged Union veterans took advantage of the expanding American railway system to grab free rides on freight trains headed back to their homes in the north. For a time, the railroads welcomed the veterans as heroes, but that generosity did not last.

That fall, as the two men neared home, small town authorities in Wisconsin swarmed their box car and arrested Taff and Goldwater and a few others for what they called "vagrancy."

Still in their Union uniforms, the two men were chained to other miscreants and marched from farm to farm where they were ordered to help harvest crops they had never grown.

The injustice rankled Taff, a farmer himself, and Taff made trouble over it. The guards beat him and then clubbed Goldwater for butting in. The fight gave the authorities an excuse to impose additional sentences past the original thirty days.

By this time, Goldwater was desperate to get home to Rosalie and their three small children. He had no way to communicate with her or anyone else, as the authorities confiscated any mail he tried to send.

Since Taff was single, the two conferred and decided that Goldwater would be the one they would free when and if they got the chance.

Soon after, when his chains came off for a moment in a field, Goldwater high-tailed it for a nearby cluster of woods. The last thing he heard behind him was Taff shouting for Goldwater to run as Taff tackled the guards.

After a few more adventures on the road, Goldwater finally made it home to Ojibwa City and to Rosalie. Since he couldn't re-cross state lines to Wisconsin without risking re-arrest, he sent his friend Silas Dropo along with a cash bribe to free Taff.

The next week, Dropo came back with the good news that the bribe was successful. The week after that, the mailman delivered a brief note from Taff:

Dear Pal Goldwater,

Thanks!

I knew I could count on you.

Yure Frend,

Taff

This note was the last Goldwater heard from John Taff until the surprise letter from Arizona with its promise to share Taff's new Bloody Angle silver mine.

Good friends did not always stay in touch. This was the way of things.

8 U. S. Territorial Judge Arthur M. Cady

Goldwater sat next to Lamont on the ratty couch on the right side of Judge Cady's courtroom, which turned out to be Cady's personal quarters on the third floor of the Olam Arms Hotel, which turned out to be Olam's only hotel, and which turned out to be a ramshackle three-story wood structure facing an unroofed portion of the Boardwalk.

Judge Arthur M. Cady sat behind his plywood desktop, supported in this place not by sawhorses but on the seats of two unmatched and unfinished wood chairs, raw as the settlement around the building.

Despite his uninspiring surroundings, the man Cady presented a perfect image of judicial probity, thick through the shoulders and chest, garbed in a suit of rich gray wool, white-haired and white bearded, leonine in appearance and imperious in manner.

Representing the Receivership, lawyer Gentry Abbey sat on a small chair on the other side of the room. He was less impressive: seedy in his dress, balding and paunchy, with a bushy brown beard.

In the back corner sat one other man, small and meek looking. Goldwater nudged Lamont with his elbow and threw a questioning look in the man's direction.

"Oscar Lafitte," Lamont whispered. "Edits the Olam *Times*."

So far, everyone but Lafitte had introduced himself with gentlemanly courtesy. Lafitte had looked up and granted Goldwater an ingratiating smile.

Goldwater found the man's expression irritating, but from his limited experience, he supposed this affability was the way of courtrooms.

Lamont was the first to speak.

"Your Honor, sitting beside me is my client Morris Goldwater, who seeks relief from the current Receivership as it applies specifically to his mine."

"Which mine is that?" the Judge asked. His voice was a deep baritone.

"Formerly John Taff's claim," Lamont said.

Cady intoned, "And on what basis does Mr. Goldwater come to this Court seeking relief from the Receivership?"

Lamont handed to the opposing lawyer Abbey a copy of Taff's letter to Goldwater.

Abbey read the letter. He handed it to Judge Cady, who read it as well, then handed it back to Lamont.

Cady shook his head. "This is difficult," he said. "Not to mention untimely. After all, Notice of imposition of Receivership on this mine was posted months ago."

"In the *Blade*?" Goldwater asked.

"No," Judge Cady said. "In the Olam *Times*. The *Blade* has ceased publication."

Lamont glared at Goldwater. He gave a slight shake of his head, as if to say, I will do the talking.

Goldwater ignored his lawyer. "I have received no such notice."

Judge Cady shrugged. "Notice was posted the required three times. And Mr. Doyle has himself duly posted bond to guarantee that he will operate the mines for the benefit of the true owners ultimately to be determined. If you are determined to be a true owner, the benefits will flow to you. That is the way of the law."

Abbey asked Lamont, "Is that document the original letter?"

"No, it is not," Lamont replied. "It is a fair copy. But I can provide the original at any time."

"Of course you must be prepared to do so," Judge Cady said.

"As I said, I will do so in good time," Lamont said. "Although I am concerned that there have been several unfortunate incidents involving originals of documents."

Cady glared. "The Court takes exception to any such suggestion. But since you are here, you may as well make your arguments for now. Although you must provide the original before this Court will consider ruling on your client's behalf."

"That is fine for now," Lamont said. He smiled as if he held some secret knowledge the others lacked. Goldwater had no idea what that knowledge could be.

"But let us begin," Lamont said. "As the letter makes clear, before his untimely death, John Taff assigned half his claim in the Bloody Angle mine to Mr. Goldwater. Of course, Mr. Taff's claim included not only the mine but Mr. Taff's personal effects, which he kept at his mine."

"Personal effects?" Abbey asked. "What for example?"

Goldwater had been to Court in Minnesota only a few times, usually to enforce small debts to his Emporium, but this proceeding seemed more informal than any he had experienced before, not only because of the shabby hotel room surroundings, but the casual manner in which the lawyers addressed each other and not the Judge.

Lamont said to Abbey. "I am glad to answer your question. As part of his original Order imposing Receivership, Judge Cady seized and handed over to the Receiver Mr. Doyle not only the mine claim itself, but everything John Taff owned, including tools like shovels and picks, and including all equipment, such as sluices and boilers, as well as all Mr. Taff's personal property, like three draft horses and clothing, food supplies and even family documents."

Lamont looked Cady in the eyes. "I must add that my most thorough research has revealed no similar draconian court order in the entire history of our nation's jurisprudence."

From his seat on the couch, Lamont followed his accusation by tipping his head in the slightest possible bow toward the judge. Goldwater read it as ironic.

"The Order of Receivership makes complete sense," Abbey told Lamont. "As I am sure Mr. Lamont recalls, according to the Mining Act of 1872, grounds for terminating a claim include any use of the claim for non-mining purposes. Taff was using the mine as his personal dwelling, which is not a mining purpose."

"Fiddlesticks," Lamont said. "A brain-dead obfuscation."

Abbey arched one eyebrow. "Sir, your language amazes me."

"And a blatant self-contradiction," Lamont said. "If it were a violation for Taff to dwell on his claim, why take his personal effects as part of taking the claim? According to your own reasoning, his private letters and such were no part of his claim."

The judge hammered on his plywood desktop with a gavel so tiny Goldwater thought it must be a toy. Where had he got it? And why?

"Gentlemen, address this Court and not each other," Cady said. He said to Lamont, "Is this all you have?"

Doyle chose this moment to open the door and step through and stand inside it. He crossed his arms. The effect of his presence was immediate. By size and carriage alone, Doyle seemed to impose his dominance over the room.

Lawyer Abbey and Judge Cady glanced his way. Both wilted under his gaze. Even Lamont seemed affected. He paused a long moment before he said, "Your Honor, the least relief this Court should offer my client is the return of Mr. Taff's personal effects to Mr. Goldwater."

"Return?" Cady demanded. "Why? Is Mr. Goldwater a non-citizen like Taff was?"

Abbey spoke to Cady but glared at Goldwater. "As the Court and Mr. Lamont no doubt recall, according to the Mining Act, rights to mining claims are reserved to U.S. citizens and those who have declared their intention to become such."

Goldwater said, "I am a U.S. citizen."

"Can you prove it?" Abbey asked him.

Lamont said, "Your Honor, I object. Mr. Abbey is directly interrogating my client, who is not even sworn as a witness."

"Nonetheless," Cady said. He repeated Abbey's question to Goldwater. "Can you prove your citizenship?"

"Yes," Goldwater said. "I can. I mean, given time to write home and obtain the documentation."

Lamont snapped at his client. "You will do no such thing." He said to Cady, "John Taff submitted his own proof of citizenship. His proof did him no good, as this Court rejected it anyway. And no such requirement has ever been imposed on any other mine claimant, for example, Alexander Doyle himself, who may have started life as a citizen, but we on good evidence believe has a personal history of having waged armed rebellion against the United States."

Lamont glared at Doyle, who snorted once and smirked again as he had in the stable the other night, when Goldwater drew his pea shooter.

"Is that all?" Cady asked Lamont.

Lamont said, "My client Mr. Goldwater will offer his documentation of citizenship after your Receiver Doyle offers his, and not before."

"Feel free to take your time," Cady said. It was not clear to whom. He hammered his little gavel. "Court dismissed."

Cady glared around. "Everybody out, and make it quick. After all, these are my personal quarters."

Everyone stood and filed out. Doyle let Goldwater and Lamont pass him, then followed them through the door close behind.

The moment they all stood outside, Doyle said to Lamont and Goldwater, "You two wait a minute."

Abbey and Lafitte kept walking. In a moment, they disappeared down the hallway.

Lamont thrust himself between Doyle and his client. "What do you want, Doyle?"

"I want peace," Doyle said. "And I'm willing to pay for it."

"For example?" Lamont said.

"Five thousand dollars."

Lamont glanced at Goldwater.

Doyle added, "Just to drop this nuisance claim and go away."

Goldwater shook his head.

"Okay, ten," Doyle said.

Goldwater shook his head again. How high would Doyle go?

"What do you two want out of me?" Doyle demanded. He glared back and forth between Lamont and Goldwater. "I have the right in this. You and your pals are all greenhorns to mining. I have been hunting through these mountains for years, often broke, sometimes starving, a filthy outsider treated by townspeople and marshals alike as nothing but a dangerous vagabond. Many the time I was down to my last swallow of water, which I had to give to my mule. It was a hard life, but I do not regret it, now that it is finally paying off."

He looked past Goldwater as if remembering something. He shook his head. He said to Goldwater, "You have no idea what I am talking about, do you?"

True, Goldwater admitted to himself. He had no personal history as a prospector. But so what?

Doyle glared down. “Fifteen thousand is my final offer. Otherwise it is war without limits.”

Lamont sneered. “As distinct from now?”

Doyle shook his head in disgust. “I am too nice a fellow.” He turned and stalked his huge frame down the hallway.

Goldwater and Lamont waited until he was out of earshot before speaking.

“Interesting that he made that offer,” Goldwater observed. “He surprised me.”

“How so?” Lamont said. “It is a good bargain for him. He takes more than twenty thousand out of your mine in a month.”

“True,” Goldwater said. "But maybe he has got some other idea, or some other idea has got him.”

“I take it you mean the death of your friend Taff?” Lamont asked.

“Are there any records of the cave-in?” Goldwater asked. “From an investigation, for example?”

“Records?” Lamont grinned. “Investigation? In Olam?”

“Any witnesses?” Goldwater asked.

“One I know of,” Lamont said. “But you do not figure to get much out of him.”

“Why not?”

“It’s Doyle’s man Roker,” Lamont said.

9 The Blade

That evening, the three adults in the Sadler house were sitting at the table after dinner. Marie had put the two children to bed.

After Victor lit his pipe, Goldwater asked Marie permission to smoke again. “Please feel free,” she said. “I do.”

She then astonished Goldwater by filling and lighting her own pipe with a wood match she struck on the sandpaper side of a matchbox.

Goldwater had heard the strange story of hillbilly women smoking tobacco, but he had never seen a woman do it. What would Rosalie think?

Marie noticed his expression. “In my own home,” she answered his unspoken question, “I will do as I please.”

For a few minutes, the three sat without speaking and wafted sumptuous clouds of smoke into the air until they shrouded the entire room in a fragrant haze.

Goldwater recalled a question from his trip to the courtroom. “It’s all very strange to me,” he said. “It’s one thing to seize a man’s mine with its precious metals, but it is another thing to take a man’s boots and shirts and private letters.”

“That is a good point,” Victor said. “I have been wondering about that myself.”

Goldwater asked, “What do you suppose Doyle and Cady are thinking?”

“I have no idea,” Victor said. “Up till now, they have been satisfied just to grab the claims. I’ve never heard of them seizing a man’s pants.”

“Lawyer Lamont tells me he has likewise never heard of it,” Goldwater said. “To highlight Cady’s bizarre tyranny, he will make that a major issue in his appeal to Washington.”

“Where it will be stacked on top of all the other appeals continuing to pile up in the corner of some office,” Marie said.

Goldwater nodded. “I suppose that is what will happen.”

“You could make a fuss yourself,” Marie said.

“How would I go about that?” Goldwater asked her.

Marie exhaled an unladylike gout of smoke. “Mr. Goldwater,” she said with a touch of asperity. “Surely you recall our offer your first evening here? That you should become editor of the *Blade*?”

Of course Goldwater recalled.

She went on. “You are convinced without evidence that thousands of miles away there exist authorities who will fight for you. But you will not fight for yourself.”

“Marie, that is not fair,” Victor said. “Mr. Goldwater is doing his utmost.”

“Is he?” Marie answered him. She turned to Goldwater. “Are you doing your utmost, Mr. Goldwater?”

“You are correct,” Goldwater said. “I am convinced. I will write and edit your paper. But remember, I am counting on you to set the type.”

Victor gave a single clap of his hands. “Why, that will do just fine!”

Marie rapped her pipe stem on the tabletop. It made a clicking noise. She gave a single brisk nod. “Fine, indeed,” she said.

10 Blade Number 1: Justice in Olam

Olam *Blade*
Dateline: Olam, Arizona
February 9
By Editor and Reporter Morris Goldwater

This past week, your humble correspondent had his first encounter with the fair and impartial justice available to us in our Court in Olam, Arizona.

His conclusion: The Olam Arizona Court is not fair, it is not impartial, and it is not just.

To demonstrate by contrast our own fairness, let us begin with a few kind words. This writer has never encountered anyone who more strongly resembles in his personal bearing the American ideal of a judge than Judge Arthur M. Cady. He bears an impressive head of white hair combed and coiffed to perfection. His beard is so luxurious as to suggest to the uninformed that he spent an extended sojourn in the field during our late War and was thereby rendered unable to find occasion to shave himself. Slightly portly, he gives the solid look of a man who—unlike the widows and children against whom he rules with depressing regularity—consumes so much sustenance as he desires whenever he desires. He gives off a credible impression of gravity, although that impression wears off more and more with each word which emanates from his yap.

Indeed, each word of his resembles an excess drop of stupidity falling from a soggy leaf onto the already muddy ground below.

It seems that our esteemed jurist prefers to be addressed by the sobriquet “colonel,” at least outside the courtroom, without specifying in which army of the recent war he earned this pleasant honorific.

It may be that our local jurist was one of the fortunate northerners able to cough up the statutory $300 commutation fee required to avoid conscription. We have it on good authority that such is the case. "Rich man's war, poor man's fight," many said, and not without reason.

His dipsomaniacal habits are well known to the denizens of several of our local purveyors of whiskey and beer. Olam boasts a multitude of these dens, and most of their inhabitants have developed great familiarity with his visage.

This writer asserts without equivocation that these attributes comprise the entire profluence of his Honor's honor.

This writer entered into Judge Cady's Court to press a valid and well-documented claim of co-ownership in a mine which belonged to a good man named John Taff, who fell under suspicious circumstances in a questionable mine "accident."

As an aside, it is worth noting that similar mysterious accidents and incidents continue to bedevil mine owners, sometimes cave-ins, sometimes robberies, as for example, being waylaid by unknown strangers.

Observe the case of one local named Olly Mack, knocked out and robbed only of his claim registration documents and not of the several gold Eagles he was at the same time bearing on his person. Suspicious, is it not?

Wide though the Honorable Judge Cady's beard may be, it lacks the circumference to hide his two elephantine ears, assailed by but nevertheless deaf to the cries of the dozens of starving children and destitute widows he has deprived of their hard-working husbands' and fathers' honestly acquired property.

Since our unpleasant encounter in his Courtroom, knowledgeable locals have informed us of many other grounds for distrust of Judge Cady's court.

We are informed on trustworthy authority, for example, that Judge Cady's designated Receiver for mines, Alexander Doyle, is a "bad man" who earned a fearsome reputation as "the quickest draw in Dakota Territory."

Having observed the man in person, we doubt not that Mr. Doyle has earned this well-deserved reputation via his good faith efforts towards applying his talents to the end of shooting deep holes in the hides of any men who displeased him, of which there seems to have been a multitude.

We are also informed by other sources, upon whom we in good faith rely, that Doyle once said about Olam miners who complain, "To Hell with them. No one can hurt me. I am too strong at Headquarters."

Although we are not of the poker playing fraternity, we regard the word "headquarters" as what our poker playing friends term a "tell." It is evident that Mr. Doyle was referring to Washington, DC as the "headquarters" for his noxious and nefarious scheme, a corruption we intend to explore in great detail in future issues, now that the *Blade* is up and running again.

Mr. Doyle is also credited with saying, "Give me a barnyard of Yankees and I'll drive them like sheep."

This writer supposes with good reason that when Doyle says "sheep," he means the rest of us, at least those of us who fought for the Union. We could be mistaken. We believe it fair to call upon Mr. Doyle to explain: are we the sheep to whom Mr. Doyle so contemptuously refers?

This correspondent declares that his recent Southern antagonists were brave men and nothing like sheep. We would never utter villainous words which could deprecate them or their undoubted manhood. For anyone who pretends to gentlemanliness to indulge in this falsification is to become a despicable man himself, and for certain no gentleman.

What vexes Mr. Doyle about our townspeople so much that he refers to us in such a derogatory way? And not just the Union veterans, but the Confederate veterans as well, many of whom also count themselves among local miners?

Does the exposure Doyle fears concern only the machinations of his infamous Silver Ring, or is there some other guilt which keeps him awake at night?

That is another topic for us to explore in future issues. We promise to explore it.

11 Times Number 1: Responding to the Effluvia of One Morris Goldwater

Olam *Times*
Dateline: Olam, Arizona
February 11
By Editor Oscar Lafitte

As he pens his response, this editor sits agog at the poltroonery of a neophyte, who, despite his evident ignorance and spite, now pretends to the role of practitioner of the journalist's high art.

I refer to the squalid ink droppings lately leaked from the pen of one Morris Goldwater, assuming out of generosity of spirit that this is his authentic name, who drips his venom onto the pages of the Olam *Blade*, and who complains in the *Blade* of alleged injustice in our highly regarded Olam Court, which we recognize as essential to the peace and well-being of our fledgling community.

It seems that this Goldwater comes brand-new to the practice of journalism, and like any babe, his first major product comes to nothing more than a loathsome self-soiling and accompanying effluvium.

Goldwater very apparently has yet to learn the requirements of true journalism as we honest and responsible professionals practice it.

Let us then acquaint this Goldwater fellow with the realities of courtroom disputes in these United States of America.

Of course, in every dispute, there are at least two parties. No matter which way a judge rules, at least one will leave Court unsatisfied with the result. If every disappointed litigant were to incite hatred towards the court system, the result will be pure anarchy, as practiced in many non-Christian lands, as we surmise that the non-Christian Mr. Goldwater would prefer.

We honest and responsible professional journalists understand that to complain of every Court result is to invite violence towards its Officers.

Although he is new to journalism, the dastardly Goldwater must know full well that result and without doubt intend it.

We therefore infer also without doubt that the scoundrel Goldwater intends by his ravings to encourage violence. If so, so be it. That will be fine.

As long as this charlatan scallywag is also aware that whatever one sows, one also reaps, and he who sows the wind, as wrote the ancient Psalmist, will “reap the whirlwind.”

12 Olly Mack

When Goldwater took the job as the *Blade's* Editor, it was not just to fight his personal war with Doyle, but to repay the Sadlers' generosity.

He had tried clerking for one day in Victor's store, but in an entire ten-hour shift, only two customers wandered in, and they bought nothing. Clerking would not repay the Sadlers. If the Sadlers wanted him for their editor, then he would have to edit.

And write too, it turned out.

Although as she promised, Marie set the type and ran the press. The real surprise was Roland, who scampered forward to gather and sort the printer's output into a neat pile of one-page sheets.

The sheets thrilled Goldwater. True, he had produced only a one-sided page with no advertisements. It looked more like a printed letter than a real newspaper. The "*Blade*" Masthead took up almost half the page.

Nevertheless, Goldwater was pleased. He had never written for publication before, only a few ads and announcements for his Emporium in the local Ojibwa City rag.

And the circulation surprised him. People snapped the few hundred copies off the tables and bars where he left them. Hundreds of pennies and nickels made their way into Sadler coffers.

Oscar Lafitte's response in the *Times* appeared soon after. That night after dinner, the Sadlers and Goldwater sat around the table talking about it.

"There's one thing which caught me off guard," Goldwater said. "I mean, his threatening language."

Victor said, "After everything you've seen in Olam, a few harsh words surprise you?"

"Lafitte put his threats right out in the open," Goldwater said. "If something happened to me, he would be the first man the authorities would look at."

"What authorities?" Marie asked.

"Good point," Goldwater conceded.

Marie added, "And after any authorities who happen to take any interest have seen and talked with that craven little weasel Lafitte, they will know he is no personal threat to you or to anyone else. Have you seen him?"

"He was in court with us," Goldwater said.

Victor said, "He is but a mouse that roars."

Experience had taught Goldwater better. "Yet they call the Colt the great equalizer."

Marie said, "Any true threat comes not from Lafitte but from Doyle and Roker. You do understand that, don't you?"

"Of course," Goldwater said.

That night, Goldwater lay awake for a while in his cozy upstairs bed and planned his next issue of the *Blade*.

He came up with an idea which appealed to him. In his first issue, he had promised to expose Doyle. At the time he wrote the threat, he had no idea how to carry it out.

As he lay there, it came to him that the answer might be hidden in the John Taff personal effects which Judge Cady had ordered handed over to the Receivership. Why else seize them?

Lamont was doing his part by making their wildly unlawful seizure part of his Appeal, but the law was slow and uncertain and stupid. What this situation called for was direct action.

Goldwater had acted on his own before. Goldwater's customers in and around Ojibwa City were generally honest. He had extended credit from his Emporium to many. Almost all paid eventually, even if repayment took years, and if they could not repay in cash, they found other ways, through barter or even by working off their debts.

But there were a few who refused to pay for what they bought and rejected his polite requests with hard refusals, nasty insults and sometimes deadly threats.

Several times Goldwater had gone to a farm or business to recover an engine or other relatively expensive item. At Rosalie's insistence, he always took along his friends Joe Wilder or Silas Dropo or both. Joe Wilder was smart and reliable, and Dropo, despite his small size, was notorious for his nastiness. Dropo's mere presence often defused explosive situations.

Once, the debtor took his complaint about Goldwater's high-handed direct action to court. But the case turned out to be a vindication for Goldwater. The judge instructed the deadbeat that Goldwater's taking his own property back was permissible in the law as what the judge called "self-help."

As he lay in bed, Goldwater decided that John Taff's personal property belonged to him and certainly not to Doyle or to Cady's Court. Once again, the situation called for self-help, and Goldwater was going to help himself.

Given the small size of the town and the big mouths of its citizens, it had been easy to learn where Doyle was storing John Taff's belongings. They were locked in a basement storage room at the Olam Arms Hotel, three floors down from Judge Cady's hotel room.

But burglary was a risky business, especially in Olam. Goldwater needed a lookout. He considered enlisting Victor, but Victor had a business reputation to protect. Goldwater looked elsewhere.

That miner Doyle's roughs had waylaid and robbed of his claim registration document seemed a prospect.

At 10 AM the next morning, Goldwater armed himself with Marie's description of Olly Mack and went looking. Goldwater asked a few questions around town and found Mack sitting at a table in the back of the Easy Money Saloon on the Boardwalk.

Even at 10 AM, the Easy Money was already half-full. Goldwater recognized Mack from Marie's description. He was a fat little bald man with a wiry brown beard. He was sitting alone at a back table nursing a whiskey bottle and a small glass. As Marie promised, he wore his trade-mark red checkered shirt. According to Marie, he was never seen in any other.

Mack glanced up and saw Goldwater coming. "Mr. Goldwater," he said. His voice was hoarse and his accent a deep-southern drawl which sounded like he had learned it growing up in Mississippi.

Goldwater asked, "You recognize me?"

"You are famous." Mack said. His 'ess' sound seemed a little slurred for 10 AM.

"Why ever has fame touched me?" Goldwater asked.

"You have the sand to write what everyone else is thinking," Mack said. "And what drew my personal attention was your mention of my name and situation."

"I merely wrote what I believe," Goldwater said. "And I felt I could not write about Doyle and his high-handed ways without also writing about you. Or did I step over a line? If so, my apologies."

"Not at all," Mack said. "I appreciate the mention." He gestured toward the bottle on his table. "Because of you, miners have been buying me drinks for days. Please have a seat." He stuck one leg under the table. A chair scraped the floor as he pushed it a few feet away.

Goldwater sat in the offered chair. He yanked it and himself toward the table. “I only heard part of your story,” he said. “I do not know all the details. If you like, I can write more about you.”

“Good,” Mack said. “Let me fill you in. Meanwhile, may I offer you a drink?”

“Ten AM is early for me,” Goldwater said.

“I respect that,” Mack said, and poured himself two fingers. He added, “You should not suppose me a weak man to have succumbed to those thieves as I did. At the moment of the attack, I was at a slight disadvantage.”

“How so?”

“I was a couple of sheets to the wind,” Mack said. He sighed.

“Only two?” Goldwater asked.

“Maybe three,” Mack admitted. “Or as they also say, a bit under the weather.”

Goldwater asked, “How many sheets are you under right now?”

“No matter,” Mack replied. “Although the clouds gather.” He looked up. “The point is that it took two men to roll me.”

Goldwater asked, “Kicked and rolled, you mean?”

“How did kicking enter into my predicament?” Mack asked.

“It is an expression I heard on the road,” Goldwater said. “Sometimes, before they rob a man, they kick their victim to make sure he is only drunk and not dead.”

“To a cut-throat, why should that matter?” Mack asked. “If he seeks only to take off you whatever you have on you at the moment?”

“A sensible question, I suppose,” Goldwater admitted. “And exactly what did you have on you at that particular moment?”

“Three Gold Eagles and a few greenbacks and a document proving registration of my claim,” Mack said.

“They ignored the cash and took only the registration?” Goldwater said.

“Which was very considerate of them,” Mack said. “Or foolish.”

“Why foolish?”

“Their apparent generosity, or perhaps it was slovenliness in their trade, is the reason I continue to possess the cash I need to sit here in the White Money and occupy my day drinking,” Mack said. “Doyle offered me a job working my own claim for starvation wages, but I possess sufficient funds to turn him down, at least for a while longer.”

“Why do you suppose your attackers made that mistake?” Goldwater asked.

“It happened that another man surprised them,” Mack said. “And, before they could finish me off, they ran away.”

Goldwater asked, “So Cady gave Doyle only your claim. but not your personal property?”

“Unlike John Taff,” Mack said. ““I saw from your writing that they took all he had.”

“Did you know him?” Goldwater asked.

“Everyone knew him,” Mack said. “And liked and respected him. A pleasant and hard-working man. It is a true shame what happened.”

“It happens that I can use some help in dealing with that shame,’ Goldwater said.

Mack asked, “With his mining claim?”

“That too,” Goldwater said. “But Lawyer Lamont is working on that for me, as he is for many others. You as well, I suppose?”

“Yes,” Mack said. “Me as well. So you are seeking aid in some other project?”

Goldwater said, "I am offering you the opportunity to participate in an enterprise which if successful may redound to your own benefit."

"How so?" Mack asked.

"It has to do with recovering John Taff's personal effects."

Mack took another sip of his whiskey. "Interesting, I suppose."

Goldwater leaned back and let the man think. Conclusions self-drawn sank in with permanence.

Mack stared around the saloon for a while. Maybe he wanted to look like he was thinking things over. Finally, he lifted his glass to his lips and tipped it and drained the whiskey. He said, "Sign me up."

"Fine." Goldwater nodded. "But the help I need must come from a sober man."

"When?"

"Tonight at 2 AM."

"Count on me," Mack said. "I will be sober—I suppose I could say 'sober as a judge'—but we know that expression does not obtain hereabouts."

"Please do not say it," Goldwater replied. "Just do it."

Mack looked Goldwater in the eyes. "I shall."

13 The Olam Arms Hotel

That night Mack showed up exactly at 2 AM, looking to Goldwater almost as sober as a legitimate judge. At least he didn't stagger.

As planned, they met in the narrow passageway between two wood frame buildings across the street from the Olam Arms Hotel. The night was cold. Thick clouds obscured the moon, a fact which would work to their advantage.

Mack huddled in the darkness close to Goldwater. He whispered, "What's the plan, Major?"

"I just need you to stand in back of that hotel across the street and act the lookout while I go in."

"Lookout?" Mack sounded disappointed. "That's all?"

"That is the entirety of your role," Goldwater said. He handed Mack an Acme metropolitan police whistle. Goldwater had been carrying one for years. He sold the product in his Emporium and had found it useful himself. The whistle he carried and had blown only once had proved more useful than the pistol he also carried but had never fired.

He had needed to blow his whistle when he witnessed a man being beaten on the street in St. Paul. The shrill squeal of the whistle drove away the attacker. If the victim had been a woman, he would have used the pistol instead.

Olly Mack fingered the little whistle. It was a tin tube about two inches long. He put it to his lips and blew. A high-pitched warble and "wheee" pierced the darkness.

Goldwater shuddered. "Please." Goldwater looked around. No one nearby. He said, "Once is sufficient for now. Follow me."

Goldwater led Mack across the street and through the narrow passage between the wood siding of Mel's Barbershop and the stone siding of the Olam Arms Hotel.

A moment later they were standing in darkness on the dirt patch behind the Hotel.

Goldwater had scouted the building's layout earlier that day. As expected, he had found a servant's entrance in back.

He told Mack, "Wait for me here. If you see anyone else going in that back door, blow the whistle."

"That's all?" Mack asked.

"That is all."

"I won't go blinky on you, Colonel," Mack said.

"That is excellent," Goldwater said. "I will keep it in mind."

Goldwater turned and crossed the dirt to the back entrance and opened the door. As he had expected, the dark entranceway led downstairs into deeper darkness. He took one stairstep at a time, feeling his way down a dozen steps until he reached the sound footing on the basement floor.

In general, Goldwater avoided depending on lantern light. If he waited long enough, his eyes should adjust to even the smallest glimmer. He stood unmoving and waited for that to happen.

After a few minutes, it did. But the darkness still seemed too deep. From his left coat pocket he took one of his paraffin-protected wood matches and a small candle he had borrowed from the Sadler house.

With his thumbnail, he scraped the paraffin off and lit the match. He used the match to light the candle.

A narrow passageway flickered before him. He stepped into it. As he walked forward, he passed doors on both sides. He stopped to turn each knob to open its unlocked door and light the space with his candle. He saw heaps and jumbles of stuff in every room, but nothing which looked like it belonged to Taff.

At the end of the hallway stood a door latched shut with an iron padlock. He shook the door latch. No luck.

In the room he had checked just before, he had seen a toolbox. He retraced his steps and opened the toolbox and grabbed a ballpeen hammer and carried it back to the padlock.

Three quick hammer blows broke the lock. But they also rang out three clangs of iron on iron.

He unhooked the broken lock from the latch and dropped it on the floor. He pulled the door open and walked in, holding his candle high in front of him.

The flickering candlelight revealed a small room about eight-by-eight feet. Trunks and suitcases and satchels lay stacked all around in careless disorder.

Goldwater bent and opened the catches on the first suitcase on his left. Nothing but a man's clothing, probably from a guest who had skipped out on his bill. Goldwater moved on to the second suitcase with the same result.

The warning "wheee" of Mack's whistle squealed from the distance. In a flurry, Goldwater picked up and pried open and dropped suitcase after suitcase, looking for any which might be John Taff's.

The whistle blew again. This time the noise of bootsteps followed. Someone was coming down the same stairs Goldwater had used, it sounded like. They were getting louder.

Goldwater spotted what he had come for. It lay in the corner, a Union haversack like his own, embossed like Goldwater's with the seal of the First Minnesota Regiment, but unlike Goldwater's, blackened with tar for waterproofing.

John Taff's, no doubt possible. Goldwater had seen the haversack too often to mistake it.

Goldwater stepped over the pile of luggage to the haversack. He grabbed it up and ran. At his first step through the storage room door he dropped his candle and stomped it out.

Fast and loud bootsteps were coming.

Goldwater had left the toolroom door open. He ducked through it and pulled it shut behind him and closed it as quietly as he could. He leaned against it and held his breath.

Heavy bootsteps passed the door and then a few steps later made a crunching noise.

"Damn," a man muttered from the other side of the door. "A candle."

The man took a few more heavy footsteps and stopped again and crunched on something new. He muttered, "My lock."

Goldwater pulled the toolroom door open and took off to the left, up the passageway towards the back entrance. He heard the man shout, "Thief! Stop!"

Two quick pistol shots hustled Goldwater along. He sprinted up the steps and out through the back door, both hands clutching Taff's haversack in front of him.

Mack had already disappeared from the backyard and soon so did Goldwater. He sprinted into the deep darkness. He did not dare use the Boardwalk fronting the street. Instead he ran behind the buildings.

For a moment, he found himself racing through a few straight piles of whitish stone low to the ground. What were they? No time to stop and find out.

Moments later, after a nightmare dash through the darkness and through the Sadler back door and up the back stairs, he was safe in his upstairs room.

He dropped the haversack onto his bed and for the next few moments bent over with his hands on his knees and gasped for breath. It had been years since he sprinted anywhere for any reason, and he had been a lot younger back then.

Goldwater straightened himself and grabbed the pitcher and glass off the bureau. He poured and drank three quick glasses of water.

His mad thirst was borne not just from his exertion but also from terror. It had also been years since anyone shot at him.

Goldwater wondered if he was still the man he remembered, though now that he thought about it, he was not sure he had ever been the man he now preferred to remember. Gunfire had scared the stuffings out of him during the War too.

One more kindness John Taff had performed was to lead Goldwater forward even in the worst moments, Taff always remained calm and composed in his duty, setting a steadfast example Goldwater forced himself to follow, if only to avoid the shame which came with cowardice and failure to support his comrades.

14 The Haversack

Goldwater sat sideways by the headboard near the top of the bed and stared a long while at the haversack.

Taff's black tar waterproofing had cracked even more than he remembered after added years of use and misuse, marching and sacking out, opening and closing, and bundling with it in a mine shaft.

Having hunted down the haversack and grabbed it and run for his life, Goldwater ended up intimidated by it.

There were privacy limits a man had to respect, even between men who slept in the same mudholes and ate the same worm-infested hardtack and marched into the same deathtraps. It was the way of things.

Goldwater stared at the haversack for a long time before he admitted to himself that there was nothing for it but to do it. He muttered a private prayer to ask God's and John Taff's forgiveness. He bent over and unstrapped the leather strips and lifted the top flap.

The first article he found was a suit of glad rags rolled up just as Goldwater had rolled up his own on his journey to Olam. Of course. After all, it was Taff himself who long ago showed Goldwater the right way to pack a haversack.

Goldwater set the clothing aside in a neat pile at the bottom of the bed.

He sorted through the rest of the haversack's contents. As he did, he separated them out in piles on the bed, as neat as he could make them, official documents in one pile, rotogravures in another, private letters in a third, and one unusual folded document as the sole item making up the fourth pile.

Goldwater read Taff's official documents first. As a young man, long before John Taff emigrated to the U.S., he had studied Mining Engineering at the University in Leipzig, Germany. Here was the German language diploma to prove it. The Diploma recognized him for highest academic honors. Of course.

Taff also kept his documentary evidence of U.S. citizenship, the very proof Judge Cady had rejected, as well his discharge from the Grand Army of The Republic after four years of service, which the certificate called "honorable" and Goldwater had personally witnessed as heroic.

Next, Goldwater looked through the personal photographs. John had kept a single sepia rotogravure of a younger version of himself surrounded by his family, including his father and mother and seven sisters and brothers.

John also kept two different photographs of a beautiful young woman. One showed the woman and Taff sitting together in front of a Christmas tree.

On the back of the Christmas picture was a note handwritten in German: "My love, when will you return to me?" She had signed it "Lisa.""

As far as Goldwater knew, John had never returned to Lisa nor she to him. But how could Goldwater know one way or the other? Goldwater had never seen John in the presence of any woman, nor had John ever mentioned women at all, outside the ordinary soldiers' banter about women in general.

But how could Goldwater be sure? The photograph was undated. Long years could have passed between the photo of this young Taff and Goldwater's meeting the older Taff in America.

Perhaps Lisa had died. Death was as normal as maggots in hard tack. It was the way of things.

But what if she had not died, at least not too soon? Goldwater hoped that the love between John Taff and Lisa had been consummated in every way possible, as Goldwater and Rosalie had finally consummated their youthful passion with mature years of marriage and children.

Now the photos raised a question Goldwater had never thought to ask. Did John Taff have a widow back in Germany? Or children? If so, how could Goldwater find them to pass onto them their rightful half-share in John's silver? Their own white money?

After Goldwater took the mine back from Doyle, of course.

The answer might hide in the private letters Goldwater had set on the bed in that third pile. He had been more reluctant to read them than any of the other documents, but now he had to.

There were only three. They were inconclusive. All were love letters written before marriage. All Goldwater learned from John's love letters was that his quiet friend had been a surprisingly passionate man.

Last came the single document in the fourth pile. Goldwater took care not to tear it as he unfolded it. It was hand-drawn, about one meter square when unfolded. At first he could not figure out what it was. Black lines crisscrossed the thick paper. German-language abbreviations notated the lines and their intersections.

After a little time and effort he recognized it. Of course. It was a schematic. For a mine. Almost certainly John Taff's own silver mine here in Olam.

With an engineer's precision and thoroughness, Taff had built his mine to last.

Of course. Taff's care and orderliness were legendary. He was never slapdash, not even in the most routine military task. His musket was always clean and his powder always dry. His meticulous attention to detail had been one reason he survived, as well as a reason that Goldwater had survived alongside him.

Goldwater repacked the haversack, taking care to replace every item in order as he had found them. The orderliness of a man as orderly as John Taff deserved no disruption.

Goldwater made one exception. He kept the schematic for himself.

Goldwater was no engineer. But he could find an engineer and show him the schematic.

If Goldwater was correct, he knew what to say in his second issue of the *Blade.*

15 Baking

Goldwater slept late again the next morning.

After waking up to two ready-made breakfasts, he had already come to expect without thinking about it that Marie would make him another. But this time, when he finally wandered downstairs, she was gone.

There was not even any coffee. When he looked in the pot, he saw a damp black pile of used grounds. The grounds gave him an idea. After all Marie had done for him, why not? There was one dish he knew how to make.

In Marie's cupboard, he found a mixing bowl exactly the right size, along with a small bag of baking flour. He set the bowl on the stovetop and poured in a bunch of the flour. He grabbed several handfuls of grounds from the coffee pot and threw them in on top of the flour. He added what he guessed was roughly the right amount of water. He molded the result with his hands until it reached the consistency he recognized from his years in the field.

Of course, he had no use for yeast.

He took a baking sheet from her cupboard and laid it on the table and spread the dough around on it. He used his pocket Barlow to cut the dough into chunks about three inches square. With his knife tip, he poked dozens of tiny evenly spaced holes in the squares. He shoved a little more fuel into the oven and lit it. He slid the baking sheet onto the rack and closed the oven door.

He walked into the dining room and took a pen and inkwell and several sheets of paper from a drawer of the bureau. He came back into the kitchen and sat down at the kitchen table. He began to scribble out his next *Blade* article.

He was still writing about ten minutes later when Marie came in from the outside.

Roland came in with her. He ran past Goldwater without a word, his face red and pinched.

She took off her winter coat and hung it on the wall hook.

“I was out looking for Roland,” she said.

“And you found him,” Goldwater said.

“Thank goodness,” she answered. “Is something baking?”

“You have been feeding me so many magnificent meals, I thought I should whip up at least one lesser meal for you.”

She walked to the stove and bent and opened the oven door. She peered in. “What pray tell are those?”

“The standard recipe.”

“They don’t look quite finished,” she said.

He said, “Soon, I hope.”

“How long are they supposed to bake?”

“I don’t know,” he said. “We never baked them in an oven. We made do with an open fire.”

“I see,” she said. “Well, I will leave that to you.” She closed the oven door.

“I go by feel and look,” he said. “It works fine.” He added, “Usually.”

“And often for me as well.”

She sat at the table. “I heard you last night,” she said. “Sometime after 3 AM. Sneaking up the back stairs.”

“I strove to be quiet.”

“Yet you were out of the house,” she said. “I won’t ask the reason.”

“Thank you.”

“But I feel I must warn you that I hear everything that happens in this house,” she said. “I have to. I lie awake most nights.”

“For what?” he asked.

"For worry," she said.

"Worry? About what?"

"Nothing in particular," she said. "And everything in general. For so many years I worried about my late husband and my late brother. Life fulfilled every worry. And I have also had Victor and Roland and Charlotte, and now you, to worry about."

"I will come out fine," he said. "You may leave me off your worry list."

"But I cannot," she said. She smiled a sad smile. "Now."

"Is there a boarding house in this town?" Goldwater asked.

"There is one," she said. "The widow Smith runs it. But with so many newcomers coming all the time, she is always full up. Men double up and even triple up in her beds. I doubt you will find a comfortable space there."

Goldwater nodded. He had learned the same on his own.

"And I think it were better for you to stay with us," she said. "I mean, since you are editing the *Blade*."

"I am too much trouble."

"Oh," she said. "You are no trouble. Especially now, since you have taken up baking."

"I must earn my keep."

She shook her head. "But I confess that I save Roland for my greatest worrying. He is a very unhappy little boy since his father died. And he was already without a mother. We have no school in this town yet, and I try to teach him myself, but he pays me no mind. He cannot sit still long enough. Charlotte seems already more advanced than he, at least in her comportment. I really don't know what will become of him."

Neither did Goldwater, so he said nothing.

She sighed and smiled another sad smile. "Meanwhile, there is good news. I sold a little advertising space in *The Blade*."

"Really?" he asked. "That is astonishing. To whom?"

"I sold a small two-line entry for Mel's Barbershop. I think he must be worried about his competitors."

"Mel has a competitor?"

"Every wife of every miner is Mel's competitor," she said. "And what is even better, I sold an entire one-page ad to our dentist Dr. Hathaway."

"There's a dentist?"

"Yes," she said. "Only one. Women shy away from their men's teeth. Unlike home haircuts, home dentistry leads to marital discord."

Goldwater asked, "If Hathaway is the only dentist, why does he need an advertisement?"

"To let everyone know he is here."

"For that he needs a full-page ad?"

"He wants to support the *Blade*. He loved what you wrote. Called it 'just dynamite'."

Marie looked Goldwater in the eyes. "The first time I saw you, I couldn't imagine how such a dilapidation of a man could write anything literate, much less edit a newspaper. But then I heard you speak. And now I know from your first effort that Victor's original judgment was altogether correct. He has that instinct about people. You are an excellent writer."

"Thank you," Goldwater said.

She said, "And, like our dentist Dr. Hathaway, I admire the way you set your nitro under the posteriors of Doyle and Cady and their gang."

Her words pleased Goldwater almost too much. He had to ask. "So you enjoyed my first issue?"

"You know I did," she said. "Very much so."

"Then you will enjoy my second issue more." He stood and walked to the stove and opened the oven door. He glanced in and said, "My confection is complete."

He grabbed a towel off the rack on the wall. He wrapped the towel around his left hand as an oven mitt and slid the rack out of the oven. He picked up the baking sheet and laid it on the stove top. He slid the rack back in and closed the oven door.

She rose and walked to his side and looked over his shoulder.

He asked, "Would you like to be the first to sample my creation?"

"I'll grant you that privilege," she said.

They stood side by side and waited for the crackers to cool. For the moment, they were comfortable housemates. He knew she felt it too. Against some part of his judgment, he let this happen.

A few minutes later, he took his first cracker off the tray and put it in his mouth. He allowed the cracker to soak a few minutes to soften it. Then he bit in.

Sandstone. Pumice. Granite.

He smiled. "Exactly as I remember."

Marie's standing there kept him from adding, "But I miss the piquancy of the maggots."

She reached out and took one cracker in her hand. She nipped a crumb off its edge. It was the smallest bite he had ever seen, a bite so ginger only a woman could have taken it.

She blanched. Then she shuddered. She asked, "You ate these?"

"Every day," he said. "Sometimes nine or ten a day."

"Why?"

"Hard tack was often all we had," he said. "And we benefited from the coffee grounds we baked into it. I predict that you will enjoy their beneficial effects yourself for the entire remainder of your day. I promise you will bask fulfilled in the lively spirit of wakefulness they will impart, especially as your experience will proceed unencumbered by the even livelier experience of battle."

"I look forward to the benefits of which you speak," she said. "But I also hope we can all go without the lively experience of battle."

She frowned. "Although I cannot guarantee it in Olam."

16 Heading For The Money

That night, as he inhaled a deep draft on his after-dinner briar, Goldwater felt as relaxed and comfortable as he had felt since his quiet evenings back home with Rosalie and the children.

Maybe in part because, this time, Marie was letting Roland and Charlotte stay up too. The children added a domesticity which reminded Goldwater of the best side of life at home.

It helped that Victor had brought out a bottle of a mellow bourbon to share with Goldwater.

Marie noticed Goldwater's expansive mood. "Victor," she said. "Mr. Goldwater seems very satisfied with himself this evening."

Victor nodded, holding his pipe by the bowl, with the pipestem in his mouth. "I see what you mean."

"Why not?" Goldwater answered them. "I sleep in a warm dry bed. I eat three squares. This is very heaven. And the evening's spirits are a special treat."

He played up what he said by taking another sip of his whiskey. The liquid warmed his insides as it went down. "Ambrosia," he said to Victor.

"I have the impression that you lived well enough in Minnesota," Marie said. "At least before the Panic."

"Yes," he said, "Before the Panic." He nodded. "But…" Unsure he should or could explain, he paused. He held his pipe by the bowl and stared down into it. The small fire still glowed red within the brown tobacco. He felt everyone's gaze on him. A bit of silence followed.

Victor and Marie seemed comfortable with the silence, but Roland broke it. "But what?"

"Indeed, but what?" Goldwater answered him. Roland's face glowed also, dark and intense. The stricken face of a lonely boy. Was there something he could do for Roland?

It is hard enough to raise your own sons, much less other people's. But Roland had no father.

Roland shared his new home with Victor, but as good a man as Victor was in other ways, he seemed to show only small interest in Roland. Victor was a bachelor and seemed something of a boy himself, little inclined or equipped to help this other younger boy Roland grow into a man.

Until you have a child, you are a child. So Goldwater believed.

"You said 'but'," Roland insisted. "'But' what?"

"Well, Roland," Goldwater said. "I will tell you but what. My dilemma began with my friend John Taff's letter. You know about that, yes?"

"No," Roland said. "No one tells me anything."

Goldwater told the entire story of the letter to Roland, who listened with a somber expression.

"So I faced a dilemma," Goldwater said. "The letter came from a man I would trust with my very life, in fact, a man I have trusted with my life under the most hazardous circumstance. His letter promised great wealth, but I had to travel more than a thousand miles through perilous terrain to reach that wealth. And I would have to leave my wife and our children and my business. I could take little of our money with me."

"Not even some?" Roland asked.

"I am a man responsible for wife and children. They also need money, if only to live," Goldwater said. "I had to leave most of my pitiful supply of cash in the hands of my wife, for any emergency which might come up, for her survival, and for the survival of our children."

He glanced at Marie, who stared at him with dark eyes, solemn and curious.

Goldwater spoke to those eyes. "Rosalie and I decided together. I would take with me some piddling amount of cash for pin-money."

From Marie's lap, Charlotte asked, "Why do you need pins so much?"

It was the first time Goldwater had heard Charlotte speak.

"This is just an expression," Marie explained to her daughter. "By pins, he means any little item one might need to buy."

Charlotte nodded. She understood. Smart girl.

Goldwater said, "I could not afford train fare, so I decided—" He paused and let the silence happen. Perhaps he had strayed into forbidden territory.

Marie prompted him. "You decided what?"

Goldwater said, "Against Rosalie's advice, I decided to resume my previous ways as a knight of the road."

Roland asked, "A knight? Like Sir Launcelot?"

"Nothing like Sir Launcelot," Marie told him.

"To make matters plain," Goldwater said, ""I jumped a freight."

He read Charlotte's confusion. "I mean, I rode the train in a boxcar, not in a passenger car."

"Why a boxcar?" Charlotte asked.

"It is free," Marie said to her. Marie asked Goldwater, "This is a thing you have done before?"

"Yes, to get home after the War, and many times during," Goldwater said. "We called them our Poor Roads of Travel. Trains and their tracks have been multiplying since their invention. By the time of the War, one could reach almost any town or even village by walking along railway tracks, so we walked them. Then one of the more clever among us realized that it was faster and easier to ride on the train itself than merely to hike along its tracks. Soon, the rest of us followed his example."

Marie turned to Victor. "Have you done this thing?"

Victor shook his head. "No. I lack Mr. Goldwater's daring. But I know it is common. Hoboes do it all the time."

"I know about hoboes," Marie said to Victor. She turned to Goldwater. "is it legal? To ride a train without paying your fare?"

"Decidedly no," Goldwater said.

"Is it dangerous?" Roland asked.

"Decidedly yes," Goldwater said.

"Why?" Roland asked.

Goldwater said, "For example, there is the weather. I have to make the entire journey, usually outdoors, or at least in an unprotected boxcar, regardless of heat or freezing rain or winter snow. On my journey here, I spent December exposed to the most brutal elements. Minnesota was cruel, and Dakota Territory downright nasty. Then in North Platte, Nebraska, a blizzard stranded us."

"Us?" Marie asked.

"I picked up a traveling companion along the way," Goldwater said. "In Dakota Territory. Like me, he was headed south. Spending winter in warmer climes is a common hobo practice. We agreed we would travel safer together than alone."

"Who was he?" Roland asked.

"His name is Crip Mick," Goldwater said.

"Crip Mick?" Marie asked.

"Some time ago he lost his foot falling off a coupling," Goldwater said. "The wheels crushed it. And he is Irish. He acquired the monica naturally."

At Marie's puzzled expression, Goldwater explained. "In the world of hoboes, no one goes by his original name. Everybody gets his moniker, or as we call it, his monica."

"What is your monica?" Marie asked.

"Sheeny Moe," Goldwater said.

Marie burst into the first laughter Goldwater had heard from her. It seemed she could not stop. Peals flowed out of her throat as from a silver bell until she was gasping. Victor looked at her in obvious wonder and delight, as if he had never seen and heard his sister laugh before, or perhaps, it struck Goldwater, had not for a long time. Hers was a hard life, no doubt, a widow stuck alone with two small children in a desert mining camp.

Some kind of dam within her had broken. She seemed unable to control the flood. At long last, she choked out, "Very courteous people, I must say."

Her surprise stumped Goldwater for the moment. Goldwater had accepted his monica so long ago, he had forgotten how strange it might seem to those new to it.

He downed what was left in his glass. "Courteous, yes," Goldwater said. "Among hoboes and tramps and bums, everyone comes as he is, naked into a new world, as if being reborn. The instant a man climbs onto a flatcar or a boxcar or onto the rods beneath, he abandons his previous life. If he boards with any pretensions, the other traveling men knock them loose, and soon. Naturally, along with his old life, the traveling man leaves behind his old name. He acquires a new monica."

"How does he choose this monica?" Marie asked.

"He does not always get to choose," Goldwater said. "Like greatness, rather than being born to him or achieved by him, his monica may be thrust upon him."

"How?" Marie asked.

"Sources vary," Goldwater said. "Some monicas are based on cities of origin, like Philly Tim, Pittsburg Jack, KC Bill, Connecticut Jimmy, and, of course, one of our champions, Slim Jim from Vinegar Hill, who never worked and never will."

Marie laughed again, not so hard, but still, it was sweet to hear.

Goldwater lifted his glass, but it was empty. Victor stretched his arm across the table and filled it from his bottle, this time to the top. Goldwater took another sip, bigger than before.

Goldwater wanted to hear Marie laugh again. He said, "And of course, I cannot omit that noble and invincible giant of a man, Syracuse Shine."

"Shine as in Negro?" Marie asked.

"Just so," Goldwater said. "We also have Frisco Shine, Chicago Shine, and Jersey Shine."

This time Marie assumed an unsmiling expression of distaste. "I do not believe I approve," Marie said. "That seems very disrespectful."

"Oh, it is disrespectful for sure," Goldwater agreed. "But disrespect towards races is not limited to disrespect towards Negroes. You have already heard my monica. We also have New York Mick, Detroit Frog, Boston Blackey—inspired by his hair, not his skin—Philly Whitey, Yellow Dick, and the Creole, Yellow Belly, who I believe wears his monica more in resentment than in honor. At any rate, he often gets quite tetchy about it."

Why stop now? Goldwater took another belt. The bourbon warmed not only Goldwater's insides but his imagination. "Another inspiration for a man's monica may be his physical limitations. We have One-eyed Jack, Detroit Shorty, Iowa Fats, Limpy Shine, and Limpy Frog. This last monica led to a beautiful rumpus."

"Because of the insult?" Marie asked.

"No insult at all," Goldwater said. "But it seems there was already another Limpy Frog. He relished the notoriety his monica bestowed and refused to share it with a newcomer to it. The two Limpy Frogs happened to collide in the same Arkansas camp. The men quite naturally came to blows. Both were injured, although not severely. While both recuperated from their minor injuries, others of the tribe held a large meeting to debate the issue and, after a spirited discussion which lasted long into the night, arrived at a resolution."

"How, I wonder?" Marie asked.

"The solution was so simple as to be obvious," Goldwater said. "It was agreed that one would be Limpy Frog Senior and the other Limpy Frog Junior."

"And that resolved the dispute, I suppose?" Marie asked. The tilt of her head and the arch of her eyebrows suggested she was beginning to suspect some of Goldwater's thumpers.

"Almost," Goldwater said. "But there was a further complication."

"Isn't there always?" Marie said. Her eyes were now merry.

Goldwater explained, "Junior turned out to be older than Senior."

"Naturally," Marie said.

"By the time everyone realized this all-too-confusing fact, it was too late. The two Limpy Frogs were on the verge of fighting it out again, this time with blades and without quarter, when other wiser heads intervened and ordered both to accept their fate as accidental sort-of-twins."

"Which they did?" Marie said. "Accept their fate, I mean?"

Goldwater nodded. "Now they are best pals. So, you see, in response to your original question, there is in fact courtesy among our knights of the American road."

Charlotte had been watching and listening to the adults talk with the usual child's mix of curiosity, confusion and indifference. But she said nothing. She was willing to wait to grow up and make sense of it later.

Roland was not. He demanded from Goldwater, "Is any of that guff really true?"

"Roland," Marie said, "Courtesy to a guest requires that we at least pretend to accept Mr. Goldwater at his word."

"Why?" Roland demanded.

"It is the way of things," Marie told him. "Meanwhile, we last left Mr. Goldwater stranded in a Nebraska blizzard. Perhaps he can move us farther along in his travels as"—she smiled at Goldwater—"a knight of the road."

17 North Platte, Nebraska

Goldwater was now the center of attention. He made the most of it. He made everyone wait while he stood and dumped his pipe ashes into the fireplace. He took a few moments to refill and tamp and relight the pipe. He resumed his seat at the table and sipped from his newly filled glass and announced, "My tale now resumes."

He said, "This Nebraska blizzard stopped every train in or out of town in its tracks. It was a storm of fantastic magnitude, possibly as great as the one our ancestor Noah experienced, allowing for the substitution of snow for rain. For three entire days and nights, no one could see ten feet in front of him or back behind him. Crip Mick and I ditched our stalled boxcar and staggered blind and freezing through the streets, desperate for shelter, until we found an abandoned house. We spent two days and nights without a morsel to eat, bundled in a basement, shivering under a pile of the rags we found and scrounged."

"Oh dear," Marie said.

"But on the third day the missionaries found us and offered to take us in."

"A blessing," Marie said.

"In some ways." Goldwater sighed. "But after our stay at the Nebraska mission, I was compelled to travel on alone, a hermit of the road, as we say."

Marie asked, "What became of Mick?"

Goldwater said, "He stayed behind at the Mission. It was angel food to him."

"Like angel food cake?" Charlotte asked.

"No," Goldwater answered. "Angel food is a sermon. A missionary preaching the Bread of Life. And miracle of miracles, on Crip Mick it worked. He got religion."

Marie said, "Or at least enough religion to make the mission a tolerable refuge?"

"Perhaps your skepticism is justified," Goldwater said, "But I was there when he testified, as they call it."

Marie asked, "You credit this testifying of Crip Mick's?"

Goldwater shrugged. "Since I expect every other man to respect my religion, I must likewise respect every other man's. And I lack the wisdom to see inside the soul of any other man, especially since I do not claim to understand my own. But Crip sounded sincere when he spoke. He had tears in his eyes. I took his conversion as the genuine article."

Goldwater glanced around the table. Both Victor and Marie seemed doubters. Roland and Charlotte were staring at him with solemn expressions.

Goldwater said, "Maybe my friend Crip Mick was just another 'mission stiff', as we call them, running a graft in exchange for winter food and shelter. Perhaps spring will melt away his religion as it melts away the snowdrifts of January. But last I saw him he was working for God."

"Working for God," Marie repeated in a murmur. Was she sincere or mocking?

Goldwater said to her, "In the end, with advancing age and the loss of his foot, maybe he had to retire from his life on the road."

He added, "It's a better choice than the black bottle."

"What is the black bottle?" Marie asked.

"Many traveling men believe that hospitals will dose them with poison from a secret black bottle."

"Why would hospitals do that?" Marie asked.

"To kill off those who refuse to follow the same settled path as the rest of humanity," Goldwater said. "Terror of the black bottle is the reason a traveling man will refuse to enter any hospital under any circumstance, no matter how sick he is. He is sure that doctors and nurses will force him to drink from a mysterious black bottle filled with poison which will kill him."

"How strange," Marie said. "And sad."

"Yes," Goldwater agreed. "It is."

Roland glared first at Marie, then at Goldwater. "So you left Crip Mick in Nebraska?"

"I was tempted to remain at the Mission with him," Goldwater said. "I confess that each day weakened my resolution to abandon the comfort of the Mission for the brutal perils of the outdoors. And the chief missionary Mrs. Olson was a kind and forgiving woman. I supposed she had to be. Though not all missionaries are."

Marie said, "But in the end you left."

"I must have," Goldwater said. "After all, here I am."

Marie persisted. "What convinced you to leave?"

Goldwater's response was simple. "I kept remembering my dear friend John Taff and my obligations to him and to my own family."

But this was a lie. Goldwater had dawdled in the Mission for three blessed weeks before he forced himself to move on toward Olam.

And no wonder. By accident he found himself in a warm house where kind local ladies served him hearty meals three times a day. Except for the Christian praying, from which the good-hearted and open-minded Mrs. Olson excused Goldwater as a Hebrew, the little one-story building was an oasis of peace.

Indeed, the North Platte Mission was the sweetest refuge Goldwater had known in years. In its warm embrace, beyond his exemption from the travails of the open road, he endured none of the tedious daily obligations of his own home—no frustrating mercantile labor in the Emporium, no inventory to count, no shelves to stock, no deadbeat debtors, no voracious taxmen, nothing to vex him in any way, not even his six loveable but often tiresome children, as demanding as baby birds in a nest, wide open beaks thrust upward without pause toward him and Rosalie.

So what had finally pushed Goldwater back out and onto the road? Of course, one part of the reason was his tortured remembrance of his real life and the real people he loved and was obligated to care for, but as much as anything else, it was Crip Mick's fervent conversion.

The instant after Mick's baptism, the man shunned Goldwater as a despised heretic. Mick was a convert in the worst meaning of the term. He was determined to show those second-rate other Christians what a first-rate Christian looked like. He never shut up about what a terrible sinner he had been, as if he were the only sinner and in fact the worst sinner who ever lived, whose sins put all other sinners' sins to shame by comparison. He was bent on winning the competition of being the worst loser.

Crip's overbearing zealotry left Goldwater alone and bored, with no one to talk with and nothing to do, not even enjoy an occasional beer at a local saloon, as even a hint of alcohol on his breath meant that Mrs. Olson would lock him out of her all-dry mission.

Mrs. Olson was the first to suggest to Goldwater that he leave. One evening after dinner, she took him aside and said, "Mr. Goldwater, in all sincerity I do not believe our Mission is the ideal place for you." With a kind smile she handed him five dollars "for the road."

There had been nothing noble in Goldwater going back on his path to Olam. In fact, his three-week vacation from real life and his reluctant departure left him disappointed in himself. But why share that failure with these good people?

Somehow Goldwater's glass was empty again. Victor noticed Goldwater's glance downward and refilled it.

Once again, Marie was examining Goldwater that way she had, as if she suspected things about him he would rather she did not. Her gaze penetrated. He suppressed his impulse to shudder under it.

The silence which followed left a space Goldwater was compelled to fill. "Well," Goldwater said. "Once again I traveled as a hermit. Of course, no express comes to this insignificant town. I had to change trains many times. I rode one through Colorado, where the weather was even snowier than Dakota, though not quite so cold. There I found some more luck. When the blizzard hit, I made my way forward car by car to the fireman and offered to break up coal for him. He was glad to take me up on it. I wound up standing on the tender in the full force of the wind hammering big chunks of coal into little chunks and shoveling the chunks forward to him in the cab so that he could shovel it into the engine and keep us all moving."

"So you earned your ride," Marie said. "That is commendable."

"Part of the way, at least," Goldwater said. "And the physical labor warmed me."

Marie said, "And you had the five dollars from Mrs. Olson."

"Not for long," Goldwater said.

"What did you spend it on?" Marie asked.

"Nothing," Goldwater said. "I got robbed. In New Mexico."

Marie asked, "Who robbed you?"

"Three bad actors I did not know. All were brandishing long knives."

"You didn't draw your pistol?" Victor asked.

"I had no opportunity," Goldwater answered him. "They had too much of the bulge."

Also not the whole truth. He had time to draw it, but he also had doubts about his ability to kill all three men with it, which caused him to hesitate just a bit too long.

"You had a pistol?" Roland asked.

Marie answered his question. "Roland," Marie said. "That a grown man carries a pistol on his person should hardly surprise."

"Then why can't I carry one?" Roland asked. "I keep asking, but you won't let me."

"You're too young," Marie said.

"That's right," Victor chimed in.

They were double-teaming the boy again. Victor and Marie were two grownups who harnessed themselves together to tow this stubborn boy towards adulthood. But the two left no daylight between them for Roland to exploit.

Goldwater and Rosalie always left a little daylight between them. No effort was required; the gap grew naturally between two different people with different personalities and different beliefs.

Goldwater had taught his own boys how to handle guns at an early age, and his girls too. "Roland," he said, "I can show you a little about shooting. If the grownups don't mind."

Roland looked surprised. He actually smiled.

Victor and Marie looked at each other and shrugged. No matter to them one way or the other.

"Anyway," Goldwater went back to his story. "I was lucky. The thieves threw me off the flatcar. But luckily, just then the train had slowed down for a station, so I pitched forward and rolled to a stop. Nothing broken. Only a few bruises."

Marie shuddered. "You have traveled among monsters," she said.

"True," he said. "There are bad actors among the tramps and bums and hoboes. Some traveling men are tramps who just like to travel, some are bums who won't work at all, and we have our share of ruffians, thieves, outlaws, robbers, and even murderers. And not just among the traveling men. There are even night hawks, which is what we call police who disguise themselves as traveling men and search the trains at night. But there is a give-away, the visible lantern light as they open boxcar doors searching. And of course there are also bulls and shacks."

At Marie's blank expression, he explained, "By which I mean policemen and brakemen."

"So my poor husband was what you call a 'shack'?"

The whiskey had loosened Goldwater's lips one word too many. He glanced down at his glass, half full. From now on, the glass would stay on the table.

"And my man was a threat to you?" she persisted. Her eyes glowed serious and sad.

Victor sighed.

"I recall now that your husband was a brakeman," Goldwater told her. "And faced his own dangers. His was by far the most dangerous job on the rails."

"Indeed," she said.

"I hope I have not offended you," Goldwater said.

"You have not," she said. "Each must make his own way in this rough world. This I know. And I hold nothing against you personally."

"Nevertheless, I apologize."

She shook her head. "No need."

Victor inserted himself into the awkwardness, "And 'bulls' are what you call police?"

Eager to change the subject, Goldwater said, "Bulls can be the worst monsters of all. Some are friendly enough, but some will not only club you and take your cash, but they will take your freedom. That has happened to me."

"There's another thing I don't understand," Roland said.

Glad of the interruption, Goldwater asked him, "What is that, Roland?"

"How do you ride all those train cars without getting caught?"

Goldwater said, "You should recognize our game. It is hide and seek. Now you see me, now you don't. There are always places to hide on a long train. Or you can ditch the train while they search and hop on again when they have finished. We have many tricks."

He added, "Or you can ride the rods where the bulls cannot see you at all."

"What are rods?" Roland asked.

"The rods are where you choose between certain discovery and near-certain death," Goldwater said. "You see, they build railway cars from wood. Heavy loads break them down. To strengthen the cars, builders insert metal trusses beneath the floors. We call these trusses the rods. Bulls cannot see a man riding the rods. If you want to avoid detection and you possess the daring, you can lie across the rods beneath a car and ride there."

"Is that safer?" Roland asked.

"No." Goldwater shook his head. "It is the most dangerous of all. While the train moves, there is no way off the rods. You lie trapped for your entire journey. No matter how the train rattles and bounces and shakes, you must hang on. And remember, you are outdoors, exposed to all weather. Your hands freeze and your back aches and you must stay awake no matter what. If you nap even an instant, you can fall. You will be crushed to death under the wheels."

"Sounds exciting," Roland said. His eyes glowed.

"Perhaps in the telling," Goldwater told him, "Not in the doing. I rode the rods through Northern Arizona." He shuddered. "I will never do that again."

But Roland's eyes glowed in the fire light.

18 Blade Number 2: Reason For Doubt

Olam *Blade*
Dateline: Olam, Arizona
February 15
From Editor Morris Goldwater

This writer's friend John Taff was not only a good man but an educated one.

Mr. Taff studied at the University in Leipzig, Germany, one of the finest in all Europe. For his excellence in his studies, that University awarded him the Bachelor of Science degree. And it happens that Mr. Taff's science was Mining Engineering. And as it also happens, the University awarded Mr. Taff his degree *Summa Cum Laude*—the highest academic honors.

By no coincidence, this was the very education which would have guided John Taff in constructing a sound, safe, and secure mine.

This writer has viewed the hand-drawn schematic which the engineer John Taff personally prepared for the mine he named "The Bloody Angle," undoubtedly as a tribute to all his fellow Americans who suffered in that hell on earth.

The writer has shown John Taff's schematic to others who are also familiar with and expert in the science of mining. Some among them witnessed John Taff's mine in person. These men verify that this was the very schematic Taff followed in construction of his own Bloody Angle mine.

Indeed, all Olam readers must be familiar with the construction technique called "square set timbering." Its inventor Philipp Deidesheimer based his life-saving innovation on nature's most sturdy structure, the bees' honeycomb.

Following the example set by nature's finest engineers, any sensible Olam miner will employ this same square set timbering technique to dig deep into our local earth with a reduced risk of collapse.

John Taff followed this same plan of successive well-supported cubes when he and his men dug his Bloody Angle mine. He shored up every floor and every level with the best support available. He was no fool.

This writer acknowledges the dangers of mining, which is perhaps the most hazardous endeavor in which modern men engage. The Divinity Himself must recoil at the number and intensity of the perils which threaten every miner every time he ventures underground.

Every day, every miner risks being poisoned or crushed or frozen to death. He may boil himself alive by accidentally striking a pocket of overheated water. Or suffocate from lack of air. The list is endless.

All these are true risks of mining. Yet none of these is the risk to which John Taff succumbed. At any rate, so we are told.

Instead, we are told it was a cave-in which killed John Taff. Thus our Honorable Judge Cady ruled after a three-minute hearing which severely tested the limits of our local jurist's intellect, comprehension and sagacity.

But in fact, the reported cave-in harbors an origin as mysterious as its sole witness, Doyle's bootlicker, pseudonymized in our town as 'Jack Roker', who appeared to us fully formed as our own municipal Athena, bearing an unknown provenance and an unknown origin, but altogether bereft of the divine wisdom of the original.

Considering all these circumstances, to put matters in as generous a light as common sense will allow, our stubborn questions and doubts must remain, clouding the air surrounding John Taff's death like the poisonous gas so often fatal to miners.

We will go further. It may be easier for a man to die in a mine than it is to die in a gunfight, but for John Taff to have died of poor mine construction was as unlikely as it would be for Mr. Doyle, by all accounts "the quickest draw in Dakota Territory" to succumb in a gun battle.

Very soon we will request that Judge Cady reopen the matter, so that the true causes of the death of John Taff can be ascertained with certainty and finality and the poisonous fumes of doubt be dispersed once and for all.

This new inquiry is the least to which the decent citizens of Olam are entitled.

19 Times Number 2: Yet More Goldwater Effluvia

Olam *Times*
Dateline: Olam, Arizona
February 16
From Editor Oscar Lafitte

Morris Goldwater is a murderer.

We admit that we lack direct evidence of this scoundrel's other crimes, but to murder a man's reputation is in our opinion a crime even more heinous than to murder his physical body.

Indeed, the discrepancy in significance between substantial loss of gentlemanly honor and mere loss of physical life is the reason all honorable men will risk death to defend their reputations.

And reputational murder is exactly what Morris Goldwater is committing as he continues to employ his worthless rag *The Blade* to excrete his foul excrudescence into the once-decent air of our fair municipality.

Without hesitation, we dare to make this accusation in a moral certainty as sure and certain as tomorrow's sunrise. To wit: without evidence, in Goldwater's outhouse sheet—for that is all that the *Blade* is, a tawdry sheet unworthy to wipe even the filthiest miscreant's foul backside—he falsely accuses a leading citizen of this town of a foul deed.

The citizen of course is Alexander Doyle, the single man who has done more than any other to bring prosperity and universal employment to our previously desolate corner of the desert.

Jack Roker is also another virtuous citizen who stands slandered and defamed by the jackanape Goldwater.

In response, we note that neither of these two slandered men is helpless to defend himself or his reputation. Far from it.

Some suggest that Mr. Doyle and Mr. Roker should go into court and bring actions for defamation.

We can accept that solution. We expect our esteemed Judge Cady to be open to any such cause of action.

But we can also suggest a quicker and more direct alternative, which would involve the direct excisement, expungement and removal of Goldwater and his nasty sheet from our town and from the entire earth.

We pray that someone will employ this solution, and soon.

20 Roland Sadler

The *Blade*'s second issue was a runaway best seller. After reading Goldwater's new article, Marie insisted on printing and setting out three times as many as before. The issue sold out in an hour.

One small incident surprised Goldwater, who did not know that Roland could even read. After snatching up the first sheet off the press, Roland pored over it and shouted, "There's a mistake!"

Marie paused her work at the press. "Whatever do you mean, Roland?"

"You misspelled a word!" Roland waved the sheet. "The word 'Angle'. You wrote 'Angel' instead. Like Bloody Angel."

"That's enough of that, Roland," Marie said. "Adults are working here."

Goldwater took the sheet from Roland and examined it. "You are right, Roland."

Goldwater said to Marie, "We have misspelled the word. It was my mistake. We had better fix this."

Which Marie did, resetting the type for that single word with the correct spelling, although it seemed to Goldwater, with a manner more begrudging than he liked.

The success of the second issue thrilled both Sadlers. They were finally bringing in some money. Marie did not need to scout for advertisers. Merchants besieged the office to purchase as much space as she could sell.

Marie predicted that the demand for advertisements would require expanding the *Blade* from one small sheet to four full tabloid-sized pages.

Their rival the *Times* also sold out. From a rumor Olly Mack passed to Goldwater, sales of the entire run of the *Times* took no more than four hours.

It seemed that Olam readers liked a good fight, the more vicious the better. And the promise of imminent personal violence only boosted reader fascination.

Goldwater's efforts as editor and writer seemed to be paying off.

Olly Mack also turned out helpful. Not only did Mack nurse a legitimate grudge of his own, but he had contacts with other miners who had suffered from Doyle's depredations and Cady's misrulings.

Some of the miners Mack introduced to Goldwater brought new evidence to support Goldwater's suspicion that the John Taff cave-in was fake. Most of this evidence was circumstantial, but Lamont told Goldwater that sometimes circumstantial evidence was powerful.

The flood of new facts excited Lamont. He told Goldwater he might be able to make a case for homicide against Doyle, Roker and even Cady. He was almost rubbing his hands in glee at the prospect. "Keep it up," he said, "And I will nail those bastards good and proper."

Lamont added, "But until then, be sure to go about armed."

Goldwater nodded. His concealed pocket pistol was something he didn't talk about. But as he considered the peashooter in his pocket, he was also thinking that he should follow his enemy Doyle's advice and carry something more powerful.

Goldwater began to notice unfamiliar men loitering near the *Blade* office. The sightings unnerved him until the morning he spotted Olly Mack as one of them.

Mack introduced Goldwater to the other loiterers, who turned out to be Mack's fellow miners. Goldwater met Vince

Dailey, Emil Haberer, Walter Hackett, and a few others, including a huge, muscular miner who bore only the single name "Quinlan."

"No need for you to worry, Captain," Quinlan told Goldwater. "We got your back."

Comforted, Goldwater went back into the house to work on his third *Blade* issue.

That evening he was sitting at the dining room table with pen and inkwell and paper, when Marie walked in from the kitchen, still wearing her coat.

She stood a moment, looking so flustered that he felt forced to ask her, "What is the matter?"

She said, "Roland has run away."

"What do you mean?"

"Just that," she said. "He has vanished."

"To where?"

"I do not know for sure. But I have my suspicions. I have searched every other place but that one, and I have yet to find him."

Goldwater asked, "How long has he been missing?"

"Since yesterday," she said. "He never came home last night."

She looked at Goldwater with an expression he had no trouble recognizing from his years with Rosalie. Although he knew the answer, he asked, "I suppose there is something you expect me to do?"

"I expect you to find Roland and bring him home," Marie said.

"Why not send Victor?"

"Victor lacks your particular experience," she said. She gave him the same look she had given him the first time they met, the look of judgment. She said, "I suspect you know where Roland has gone."

Which was true. He did know. He had seen the hobo camp just outside Olam when he ditched the freight on which he rode to town. Goldwater had taken shelter in the Sadler stable in the first place because he preferred a barn over a hobo camp.

Despite the mistaken notions of some delusional romantics, any hobo camp was a perilous place. Every camp contained dangerous criminals, and dealing with even the most civil hobo was a tricky business.

The life of a hobo nowadays was much harsher than the life of a hoeboy had been right after the War. Over the years the hoboes themselves had turned into a much rougher lot than discharged Union soldiers, who were a pretty rough bunch themselves, being combat veterans, but at least in general had started their lives as farmers and other solid citizens.

Goldwater was still holding his pen above the paper, poised to write. He set the pen into its holder. He said, "I will look into the matter."

"I can tell you where the camp is," she said.

'No need," he said. "I know the spot."

He stood and started towards the stairs.

"Where are you going?" she asked.

"Why, up to my room, of course," he said.

"Why? The camp is on the edge of town."

He looked down at himself and his respectable clothing. "I prefer to wear the same outfit I came to town in. That is the best course. It is certainly the safer one."

21 The Camp: Booze and Bromides

Rigged out in the same ragged coat and torn trousers and worn boots he had worn his first night in town, Goldwater made his way towards the railroad yard and the camps beyond.

As he walked along, a half-moon illumined all he passed.

In this part of Olam there was no boardwalk, just dirt paths which spiderwebbed higgledy-piggledy here and there among the huts and hootches and hovels spread among the low hills and shallow valleys.

A red glow shone through one greased paper window. A neighborhood entrepreneur was promising delights Goldwater had long ago decided he was better off without. Goldwater kept walking.

The sour tinkling of an out-of-tune piano plinked out of a ramshackle one-story wood frame house. It was the only dwelling in this neighborhood which boasted a wooden door. A red lantern glowed from above that door.

He passed through a section of the same low white walls he had passed the night he fled with the haversack he had grabbed out of the Olam Arms. The walls were ankle-high heaps of unshaped stones, mortarless, white in the moonlight. Men must have stacked them in those neat rows. What men, and why? The rows looked too old for the current Olam.

Up ahead, the yard's high metal water tank shone in the moonlight, a bright silvery cylinder whose teapot spout hung over the tracks, put there to deliver water to coal-fired engines to convert into the steam which propelled the trains.

Goldwater stopped by the tank. Three hoboes and a teenage boy stood around it. The boy wasn't Roland. The men were explaining hobo life to the boy, likely trying to recruit him to their ways.

Roland had probably stood in this very spot. Town boys were always lurking in railroad yards to watch the operations. The yard was the only reasonably wholesome entertainment in a desert village without a swimming hole or a theater or a library.

Once mined, all Olam's ore passed through this yard. Small cars on small gauge tracks carried it here direct from the mines. This very moment, two powerful men were shoveling loads of ore from mine cars onto the cars inscribed with the name "Arizona Transcontinental Railway." Olam lacked smelters; the Transcontinental would carry the ore to the smelters elsewhere.

Several guards patrolled, armed with ten-gauge shotguns or Winchester rifles or dragoon Colts in scabbards at their sides. Risk from trigger-happy guards was one reason Goldwater had ditched the train a mile out of town and bypassed the yard by hiking around it into town. He didn't want volatile men like these to mistake him for a thief or a trespasser.

A guard nestling a shotgun in his arms strolled over to take a closer look at Goldwater. He stopped for a moment, then called out "Mr. Goldwater," and smiled and tipped his slouch hat.

Comforting to be recognized. Local fame, though fleeting as any other, brought some advantages. Goldwater tipped his own slouch hat to the guard in acknowledgement.

Water tanks like this one were bulletin boards for traveling men. Hand-scrawled monicas and dates covered the sides of the tank: "Detroit Willy, 07-10-1872"; "Philly Frank, 06-23-74"; and the like, plus some practical hobo intelligence: "west-bound trains no good"; "bulls hostile"; "roundhouse OK for kipping"—Goldwater understood from this last bulletin that shacks and bulls would allow a traveling man to nap in the Olam railway station's roundhouse.

Goldwater imagined Roland standing in the same spot trying to decipher hobo hieroglyphs as mysterious to him as the scrolls of ancient Egypt would be. Roland would have craved the lowdown from any men around who could translate them. Some would have used the opportunity to fill his empty boy's head with thrilling tales of wondrous adventure on the road.

Angry and frustrated and feeling alone, Roland would be easy to snare for some enterprising jocker looking for a boy to snag for the next train out.

Once, back in Ojibwa City, a 13-year-old neighbor boy had disappeared and never been found. He might have wandered off with hoboes by choice, or worse, might have been kidnapped. No one knew.

There was no hope to find a boy lost that way. The thousands of miles of new track laid in the past fifteen years erased any possibility. And the new intercontinental railroad meant that the boy might have been taken anywhere in a country three thousand miles wide and two thousand miles high.

No Roland at the tank. Goldwater crossed the tracks. A few yards on the other side flowed a trickle of water barely wide enough to serve as a ditch back in Minnesota but accounted a river or at least a creek here in water-starved Arizona.

A ready water supply made this a good place for wandering men to camp, as it probably had for the Indians over the long centuries before the white men showed up to conquer it.

Another hundred yards along, Goldwater spied some trees and under them the flickering of small campfires. A closer approach revealed shadowy figures around the fires. He shouted, "Hello, the camp!" and, following the custom, walked in and squatted on the ground at the camp's outermost edge.

Together, the moonlight and the many fires lit the scene well enough to expose at least a hundred assorted men and women and children, camping in tents and lone sleeping bags, probably because they had to wait to find available lodging in Olam, or even wait for lodging to be built. Newcomer camps like this surrounded every boom town in the West.

One man was stooping to feed some pink sheets into his fire, The flames flared higher with each new page he threw in, as if the *Police Gazette's* torrid tales strengthened the blaze.

For a while, Goldwater simply sat and scanned the scene. He was scouting for Roland. He did not see him.

Goldwater stood and walked on through the camp. He passed among families of men, women and children who had set up tents near their fires, friendly groups whose members all seemed to know one another. Shrieking and laughing children dashed past and around Goldwater as he moved along.

No Roland here. But from the other side of another little creek came the glow of another lone fire lighting a smaller camp. He sloshed through the shallow water to the other side.

By the weak firelight, he counted about ten figures. It seemed all were male. Some stretched out on the ground in dark mounds, probably sleeping. A few sat up and smoked home-made cigarettes or stubby stogies. One was stirring with a stick in the stewpot hung over the fire. Two others sat off to the side and leaned against each other, passing a small bottle back and forth.

Goldwater sat on the ground again. No sign anyone noticed him. On the other side of the fire about fifteen yards away stood a figure too small to be a man. A boy, likely. He might be Roland.

Time for caution. Bad actors were common among hoboes and tramps and bums. They resented scrutiny. In fact, probably nine out of the ten men here had chosen the traveling life to avoid attention.

The boy hunched over and vomited onto the ground. Goldwater heard the retching noise even at this distance. The boy might be puking out alcohol, or worse, potassium bromide.

Goldwater sold both over the counter of his Emporium. Between booze and potassium bromide, the bromides were worse. He sold the bromides for treatment of epilepsy and other illnesses, but he knew that some of his customers dosed themselves for different ailments, the most common being misery, boredom and stupidity.

During his spell in the jailhouse years ago, Goldwater had seen prisoners slopping themselves on the bromides. It was a convict's path to temporary escape from the desperate monotony of the life incarcerated. Prisoners acquired the potions from the guards and trustees by trading whatever items of value they could scrape together, like meat scraps or tobacco shreds.

Goldwater had kept clear of the bromides, just as he avoided the toxic home-brew alcohol which prisoners fermented in the hidden recesses of the jail, often with the connivance of bribed guards and corrupt trustees.

A man-sized dose of potassium bromide could kill a nine-year-old boy as sure as it would kill any small animal.

Goldwater rose from his spot and took a few steps closer. The man leaning beside the boy with his hand on the boy's back was no doubt the jocker who had snared him.

The pairing of jocker and boy was a common custom among traveling men. Jockers snared their boys to be serviced by them. The kids did the begging and stealing and the jockers grabbed off the proceeds.

Hoboes called silver "white money." Miners gouged their white money from sullen earth. Doyle gouged his white money from abused miners. Jockers gouged theirs from damaged children.

The service of boy to his jocker included not only white money, but also the practice some labeled white slavery, as the boys sometimes serviced their jockers sexually as well.

Even though some saw this as the way of things, it was a fate truly worse than death. So Goldwater believed.

Two cautious steps more, and Goldwater could see by firelight the boy's size and shape and his dark hair. It might be Roland.

The jocker must have noticed Goldwater coming near. He turned and spat out a few words Goldwater didn't quite get, but his nasty tone delivered the message. The jocker was a big fellow. Deep grooves and bumps in his face spelled out a history of rough weather and rougher treatment by bulls and shacks and other traveling men.

Goldwater bought time by lifting his hands palms up in a mollifying gesture. But he also took two steps closer.

The boy straightened and happened to look Goldwater in the eyes. Filth smeared the boy's face. Vomit drooled down his chin. His eyes were wild.

It was Roland.

Goldwater took two more slow steps forward.

The jocker growled, “That’s plenty close,” and stepped toward Goldwater. They were only a foot apart. He drew his shiv, a thin and nasty blade which glimmered in the firelight.

Goldwater kicked him in the scrotum.

The jocker clutched himself and teetered, but he did not fall, so Goldwater kicked him again, and he toppled. For luck, Goldwater kicked him one more time on the way down.

The man fell on his back and rolled back and forth a couple of times and shuddered to immobility.

Neighboring men began to stir in the darkness. Some muttered foul oaths.

One demanded, “Did you see what that rube did to Boston Fish?”

“Hey, Rube!” One shouted. Another picked it up. “Hey, Rube!”

“Hey, Rube!” was the traditional call among traveling men to collect and thump a troublesome stranger.

Goldwater ignored the shouts. He leaned close to Roland and asked, “Do you recognize me?”

Roland stared and said nothing.

Goldwater asked again, “Roland, boy, do you recognize me?”

Awareness flickered in Roland’s face. He nodded.

Goldwater said, “It’s time for you to come out of here with me, Roland.”

Roland nodded again.

Goldwater kept his eyes on Roland, but he sensed the men gathering around them.

Goldwater extended his hand. Roland took it.

Goldwater turned to leave. Roland followed, his small hand cupped in Goldwater’s larger one.

A few men had gathered to block their way back across the creek. One stepped in front. He drawled in a Texas accent, “Where you going with Boston Fish’s punk?” He was a short man, but stocky and powerful looking. The firelight flickered over his much-broken nose.

Goldwater knew better than to kick a Texan with a much-broken nose. He pulled his revolver from his coat pocket.

Broken Nose sneered. “If you want to take that boy out of here, you’re going to have to come up with something a whole lot more convincing than that little rod.”

A shout came from Goldwater’s right. “Hey! Sheeny Moe!”

Goldwater glanced toward the voice.

The shout came again: “Hey! Sheeny Moe!”

Crip Mick limped out of the crowd and stood between Goldwater and Broken-nose.

A miracle.

If this miracle were Goldwater’s way out, he wasn’t going to blow it. He clamped his mouth shut. Let Mick do the talking.

Mick told Broken Nose, “This is Sheeny Moe. I know him.”

“So?”

“He’s good people, I tell you,” Crip said. “If he’s taking this boy, he’s got good reason.”

“Like what?”

“Maybe a prior claim.” Crip turned to Goldwater. “Prior claim, that’s right, ain’t it?”

Crip was handing Goldwater a big break. By the code of these rough men, such as it was, snaring another man’s boy was a violation. Prior claim was going to be an easier sell among these men than any sob story about some orphan’s adoptive parents. Half the men here had grown up as orphans.

“That’s right,” Goldwater said. “He’s my boy. I have the prior claim on him.”

Crip Mick turned to Broken Nose. “See? Sheeny Moe here is good people.”

Broken Nose took what felt to Goldwater like an eternity. Finally he shrugged his indifference. “Boston Fish’s just another eye doctor anyway. Why should I take a bullet for him?” He walked away.

The men dispersed as fast as they had gathered. In a moment or two, only Goldwater and Crip Mick and Roland stood together in the firelight. The others were once again shadowy lumps on the ground.

“Mick,” Goldwater said, “Maybe you just saved my life. But what are you doing here?”

Crip Mick said, “After a couple weeks at the Mission I got bored. All that praying from Mrs. Olson stretched my nerves. And I got tired of eating Nebraska snowballs. I decided to follow the birds down south, like my original plan.”

“You came a week or so too soon,” Goldwater said. “It has been cold as Pharaoh’s heart around here. But lucky for me you came at all.”

Crip Mick glanced at Roland, who stood silent and morose, staring into space. “So what’s this boy to you?”

“Friend of a friend.”

Crip Mick glanced at the jocker on the ground who was just now starting to wriggle around. “You took your chances. That Boston Fish is a mean one.”

“He is not the only mean one,” Goldwater said.

Crip Mick nodded. “Never figured you for something like this before. Where you taking the boy?”

“Home,” Goldwater said.

“Why?”

“He has one,” Goldwater said.

Crip Mick grinned. “Unlike me and you?”

“I have a home in Minnesota. And you had a home in Nebraska if you wanted it.”

Crip Mick ignored that, "I still don't savvy. What's your interest?"

"I know this boy," Goldwater said. "I will not allow him to become any man's punk."

Crip Mick said, "And I thought I was the one got religion."

"Did you?" Goldwater asked. "I mean, for real?"

Crip Mick looked sad. "Never ask a woman about her virtue or a traveling man about his religion."

"Good advice," Goldwater said. "Well, thanks again." He offered his hand.

Crip Mick shook it. "Bye, Bo."

"Bye, Bo," Goldwater replied, and walked Roland away.

22 Extrication

They slogged across the creek and made their way among the tents and fires of the bigger campground and then onward to the railroad yard and its water tank.

Roland was in no shape to take back to Marie. Goldwater had read about Caribbean zombies, a name for soulless men. He was walking a zombie boy. All he could hope was that the stupefaction would wear off. Marie was not going to appreciate Roland in his current condition. She might even give him a hiding.

Slopped stupid by bromides or booze or something else, Roland followed Goldwater without a word. He showed no sign he was aware of his surroundings. Every so often he stopped for no reason. Only when Goldwater took his hand and tugged him along did he move again.

Two hoboes stood at the water tank studying the scribblings on its side. The teenage boy was gone. Goldwater hoped he was home where he belonged.

As Goldwater and Roland passed the tank, one grizzled hobo called in a drunk's slurred voice, "Hey, kid, want some lemonade?"

Goldwater stopped and turned and glared. "No he does not."

The man grinned and said, "No need to act so high-hat about it."

Goldwater suppressed his impulse to shoot the man and turned and walked on.

When they passed through the ring of low stone walls Goldwater had passed through on his way in, Roland stopped and looked around and said his first word. It was, "Indians."

Goldwater stopped and looked at him.

"Indians," Roland repeated. "They lived here and built stone walls."

"I see," Goldwater said.

"Long ago," Roland said. "The walls were higher then. To stay safe."

"I see," Goldwater said again.

Roland nodded, as if he had made some important point. He let Goldwater take his hand and walk him along some more.

As they hiked among the shanties and whorehouses, Roland came to life a little further. He asked, "Where are we going?"

"Good question," Goldwater replied. "Right now, I have no idea. But I'm glad to see you rejoining the living again."

"What happened?"

"You do not remember?"

Roland shook his head.

"That is for the best," Goldwater said. "But from now on, do everyone a favor and avoid the railyard."

"Okay." Roland nodded. He fell back into silence.

But where to take him?

Goldwater needed help. He had met only one man in this town he might be able to rely on. Goldwater led Roland to the Easy Money Saloon and his favorite lush Olly Mack.

At this late hour, miners and other drinkers jammed the hot and stinking place. Olly sat at the same table as before. Must be his table. He spotted Goldwater and Roland as they made their way through the crowd. The big man sitting with him had his back to Goldwater. After Olly looked up, the big man turned and followed his glance to Goldwater and stood.

It was Quinlan. He stood and gave Goldwater a bear hug and lifted him off the ground and set him down again. He asked, “General, I am thrilled to see you. Can I buy you a drink?”

“Sure,” Goldwater said. “Why not? I have had a rough night.”

Quinlan turned and headed off toward the bar.

Olly raised his eyebrows. “Didn’t drink the last time you was here.”

“That was morning,” Goldwater said. “This is not.”

“Actually, it is morning,” Olly pointed out. “Who’s the kid?”

“Roland Sadler,” Goldwater said. The name was Sadler, wasn’t it? Must be.

Olly stood and extended his hand to the boy.

Roland looked a little surprised, but he shook it. His little boy’s hand disappeared into Olly Mack’s round rough mitt.

Olly gave Roland a once-over and let go of his hand and sat again. Goldwater sat too. After looking around the saloon filled with rough men, maybe to see if he was allowed to sit in this place, Roland joined them at the table. No one said a word against it.

Quinlan came back with three whiskeys on a tray, along with a glass bottle of red soda pop. He set the soda pop in front of Roland and two of the whiskeys in front of Goldwater and Olly. He laid the tray on the table and sat down to his own whiskey.

Roland looked down at his soda pop. “Wow,” he said.

“Wow?” Olly asked him.

“They won’t let me have this at home,” Roland said.

“Then you better grab your chance, kid,” Olly said. “Drink up while you can.”

He winked at Goldwater.

Roland glanced at Goldwater, who nodded. Roland grabbed up the bottle and tipped it and drank. The red liquid bubbled and gurgled as Roland emptied half the bottle on his first try. He lowered the bottle to the table and shuddered. "Good," he said, and smiled.

Olly raised his eyebrows and shook his head and lifted his glass in salute to the boy. Goldwater and Quinlan saluted Roland and drank too.

Olly must have noticed something when Roland lifted the bottle. "Say, boy," he said to Roland, "Show me your wrists."

Still a little out of it, Roland said, "What?"

"Your wrists, boy," Olly repeated.

Roland stuck out both hands and held them over the table, hands turned up.

"Pull back your sleeves, boy," Olly said.

Roland reached out with his left hand and pulled up his right sleeve.

"Now the other one."

Roland pulled back the other sleeve.

"Hot damn," Olly said. He turned to Quinlan. 'You see this?"

Ugly red welts crisscrossed both Roland's wrists. They seemed to glow in the saloon gaslight.

"What in Hell are those?" Quinlan asked.

Olly glanced at Goldwater. "You think it was lye?"

"Or crushed and dried blister beetles," Goldwater said. "Same result."

Quinlan asked, "What are you two clowns talking about?"

"The boy's jocker did it," Goldwater said. "The tramp who wanted to run him. They call those burns lye bugs. The more scarred up a boy is, the more jack he will bring in. He can sell the suckers on the notion he is a cripple."

"Plus, he'll be more stuck in the road life," Olly said. He asked Goldwater, "Right?"

Goldwater nodded.

Quinlan asked, "Will those heal?"

"Not if the jocker keeps rubbing in carbolic acid every day," Goldwater said. "That way he can keep the wounds fresh."

"Damn," Quinlan muttered. He asked Roland, "Who did that to you?"

Roland was staring at his wrists as if he hadn't noticed them before. In a voice almost too quiet for Goldwater to hear, he said, "I hurt like the dickens."

Olly said, "Roll your sleeves back down, Roland. Please."

Roland did.

Quinlan asked Goldwater, "So who was it burned this boy?"

"You can find him in that little hobo jungle just across the creek from the newcomers' camp," Goldwater said. "Nursing his balls."

Quinlan asked, "Major, you went into that hell hole alone?"

Olly grinned and said to Quinlan, "Our friend Colonel Goldwater has balls of his own."

"That's fine as far as it goes," Quinlan said. "But a couple of sore huevos will not suffice. This will not suffice at all."

He rose from his chair. He lifted his whiskey glass and gulped it empty. He slammed the glass down on the table and turned and walked out of the saloon.

Olly winked at Goldwater. Then he said, "Roland, I better take you home with me. Violet will come up with something for those wrists of yours."

"Violet?" Goldwater asked.

"My wife," Olly said.

Goldwater had not considered that Olly might have a wife. "News to me," he said.

"You'll see," Olly said. He stood. The other two followed Olly out of the saloon. They walked down the Boardwalk and then off the street and onto the hard ground toward the same shantytown Goldwater and Roland had passed through before.

The three walked along a few minutes in silence, until Goldwater asked Olly, "Does your wife mind you spending so much time at the Easy Money?"

Olly stopped and faced Goldwater. "You got a wife?"

"Yes."

"Where is she?"

"Back in Minnesota."

"Does she mind you being eighteen hundred miles away all these weeks?"

"She understands that I have come for a reason," Goldwater said. "My journey may lead to a bonanza for our family." But his excuse seemed feeble even to himself.

Olly led them past some shanties to his shack on a low hill. He lifted the latch on the front door. Goldwater and Roland followed him inside.

To Goldwater's amazement, Violet Mack turned out to be a young-looking woman, slender as a wand despite the eight children she had borne so far, and lovely in face and form to boot.

Maybe it was the eight kids which drove Olly to the Easy Money. It sure was not Violet.

When Violet saw Roland's condition, including his wrists, she clucked and scolded and forced Roland to take a bath. After he toweled himself down and dressed himself in the new hand-me-downs she dug out of a big trunk, she slathered his wrists with a cure-all from a bottle labeled "S.B. Goff's Magic Oil Liniment" and forced him to drink from a brown bottle labeled "Dr. J. Townsend's Sarsaparilla."

Goldwater sold neither cure-all himself, though his wooden store shelves bent under the poundage of all the popular ointments, salves, and patent medicines he did carry, like

White Cloverine Salve ("compounded from a physician's prescription"); Cuticara ("a positive cure for every form of skin and blood disease"); and Gentry Brothers Famous Mange Remedy ("A Delightful Human Head Shampoo and Tonic").

Goldwater had discovered the hard way that if his Emporium did not stock remedies like these, he would lose otherwise loyal customers to merchants who did sell the twaddle.

Much to Goldwater's surprise, the liniment on Roland's wrists actually soothed his pain, or so he claimed, but the "sarsaparilla" seemed to stupefy him almost back to intoxication. Goldwater sniffed the cork. The main ingredient turned out to be alcohol.

Despite his mild inebriation, Roland now seemed presentable. He was once again a clean little boy in clean clothes. And Roland had suffered long enough, at hands both maleficent and beneficent. Time to take him home.

Goldwater and Roland thanked Olly and Violet and made their way through the darkness back to the Boardwalk and to the Sadler house.

When Marie saw Goldwater pull the reluctant Roland through her front door, she launched a flood of grateful tears and mighty hugs. She created a scene dramatic to the point of being overwrought. Her display embarrassed Roland. He stood stiff and awkward in her embrace.

As far as Goldwater was concerned, Marie's show served Roland right. But some part of him wondered whether her display was genuine or somehow forced. No way to tell with this woman. She seemed to swing back and forth from one feeling to its opposite.

Maybe Roland would learn a lesson after his narrow escape from disaster, but Goldwater doubted it. His own kids never did.

23 Cady's Courtroom Another Time

When Goldwater came into court, Oscar Lafitte flashed a friendly smile, as if the two men were partners in some amiable joint enterprise, which to Lafitte's thinking seemed to include agitating for Goldwater's murder. It struck Goldwater that Lafitte entertained a broader definition of amiability than Goldwater did.

Once again, Goldwater sat next to lawyer Lamont on the same ratty couch on the right side of Judge Cady's cramped courtroom, venued as before in the judge's hotel room on the third floor of the Olam Arms.

Likewise just as before, Judge Cady was seated behind his plywood desktop, Lawyer Gentry Abbey represented the Receivership from the couch on Cady's right. and Lafitte squatted again on his chair in the back corner.

Judge Cady still looked magnificent and judicious and authoritative. He stared into the corner with a morose expression. When the scraping of chairs died down, he swiveled to face the room. He gave a rap of his fingerling gavel on his plywood desk and proclaimed, "This Court is now in session."

Lamont said, "Your Honor, I appear once again to represent Morris Goldwater, who moves the Court to reconsider its original ruling that his partner John Taff's death was a death by misadventure and not the homicide it surely must have been."

Cady asked, "On what grounds does Mr. Goldwater make his motion?"

"On the grounds that the original determination was founded on an incomplete understanding of the facts."

"Really?" Cady raised both bushy white eyebrows. "Which facts?"

Abbey said, "The Receivership objects. Goldwater's claim lacks the required ripeness to be heard."

"Ripeness?" Lamont said. "What does that mean?"

Abbey sneered. "Since the less-than-learned Counsel seeks an explanation, I will provide it. The ripeness doctrine prevents federal courts like this one from entangling themselves in abstract disagreements by adjudicating disputes too early for pertinent facts to emerge."

"I know the doctrine," Lamont said. "But I see no application of that doctrine in this instance."

"All the facts have not yet emerged," Abbey said.

"That's why we're here," Lamont said. "To emerge them."

"The case is also moot," Abbey said. "Perhaps the Court may deign to explain the mootness doctrine to Mr. Lamont. In any case, I will do the job. A matter is moot if further legal proceedings with regard to it can have no effect, or events have placed it beyond the reach of the law. Thus the matter has been deprived of practical significance and rendered purely academic."

Lamont shook his head in disgust. "You just said the case isn't ripe because we brought it too soon. Now you're saying it's moot because we're too late. Which is it?"

"Who is to say?" Abbey smiled a condescending smile. "Perhaps both."

Lamont snapped out, "Neither, you mean."

Abbey plowed ahead. "There is also the issue of standing. Mr. Goldwater lacks standing to bring this motion."

Lamont snapped back, "Of course Mr. Goldwater has standing. He was partner to John Taff. This is yet another trivial contention."

"It is not at all trivial," Abbey said. "Assuming Mr. Goldwater can ever establish his claim to Taff's mine, he will himself be a beneficiary of the Receivership, which after all operates only to benefit all miners. So, he is making a claim against himself, which is nonsense, ipso facto."

"Ipso facto?" Lamont demanded, the outrage obvious not only on his face but in his rising voice. "What does that mean?"

Abbey said. "If Counsel does not recognize the Latin, it is not my role to educate him. It is his prerogative to study and learn, should he possess the will and the wit."

"Oh, I recognize the Latin," Lamont said. "It is any bizarre potential application of this antediluvian foreign phrase to the current case which I question. I do not believe that the learned counsel knows what the phrase means or, assuming he knows that much, how it could possibly apply to this case."

Abbey opened his mouth to speak, but Cady cut him off with a rap of his tiny gavel. "Gentlemen, that's enough of this niggling and haggling. I will take the questions of ripeness, mootness, and standing under advisement. Please proceed." He nodded to Lamont.

"Thank you, Your Honor," Lamont said. "Mr. Goldwater has evidence he wishes to present to the Court."

"Is this new evidence?" the Judge asked.

"Yes, Your Honor," Lamont said.

"Your Honor, I once again object," Abbey said. "Goldwater had his chance to present this so-called evidence at the initial hearing on this matter."

"Mr. Goldwater had not even arrived in Olam yet," Lamont said. "And as I said, this is new evidence, so he could not have presented it even had he been here."

"This makes no sense," Abbey said.

"You make no sense," Lamont replied. His neck was reddening more with each Abbey interruption.

"I will try my sense against yours anytime," Abbey said. "You are nothing but another whippersnapper."

Enough. Goldwater butted in, if only to keep his man Lamont from exploding. He spoke directly to Abbey. "That is one thing I have never understood."

"What?" Abbey asked. He glared at Goldwater as if he resented being addressed by a non-lawyer.

"What exactly is a 'whippersnapper'?" Goldwater asked him. "I understand that the word is a longer version of the word "whip-snapper," which as a word at least makes sense. How can anyone snap a whipper?"

"I do not trouble my head with such silly and pointless questions," Abbey told Goldwater. "You must inquire from whoever invented the word."

"Whippersnapper is a word you just used yourself," Goldwater pointed out. "Apparently without understanding its meaning. Though it is possible that the word 'whippersnapper' derives from the ancient term 'whipperginnie', an ungentlemanly term intended by its users to disparage the fairer sex."

"I don't know about any of that," Abbey said. "I certainly don't know what a 'ginnie' is. And I certainly intend no disparagement to women."

Goldwater nudged his lawyer with his shoulder.

Lamont had been sulking. He turned to Goldwater. His face was still bright cherry.

Goldwater whispered, "Abbey is just provoking you. He seeks to distract you and get you off your game. Pay no attention to the man's churlish interruptions."

Of course, since everyone in the cramped space was sitting almost in everyone else's lap, everyone must have heard Goldwater too.

Good.

Lamont nodded at Goldwater. He took a deep breath. He made an elaborate show of exhaling. He turned to Abbey and threw him a cheerful smile.

Judge Cady said, "If you gentlemen have completed your disquisition on the English language, we can proceed."

Lamont said, "Your Honor, I call as my first witness Morris Goldwater."

"The complainant himself?" Abbey said. "Really, Your Honor, this is too much."

"Too much what?" Lamont asked. He granted Abbey another cheerful smile. "Too much evidence? Too many facts?"

Judge Cady told Abbey, "As I already ruled, everything is taken under advisement. For now, I will hear what Mr. Goldwater presents."

He turned to Goldwater and handed him a Bible and asked, "Mr. Goldwater, do you swear to tell the truth, the whole truth, and nothing but the truth?"

Goldwater placed his right hand on the book and said, "I swear."

"I object," Abbey said, "How can this man who is not a Christian swear on our New Testament, a writ at whose holiness he both privately and publicly scoffs?"

"I scoff at nothing," Goldwater told Cady. "And the swearing is easy. I just swear on the part I do believe in, which is the much longer Hebrew Scriptures part at the beginning."

"That's good enough for now," Cady said. "Go ahead."

Lamont asked Goldwater about the John Taff haversack and its contents.

Goldwater explained all the personal papers he had found and what each meant. He handed Cady the schematic from Taff and explained how he had verified that the mine followed it, as he explained, "to a t." Lamont offered it into evidence.

Abbey said, "I object to the admission of this document into evidence. I want to examine this witness about this alleged schematic."

Lamont said, "You may ask."

"Mr. Goldwater," Abbey began. "Would you care to explain how you came by this alleged schematic?"

"I already did," Goldwater said. "It was in John Taff's haversack."

"Which you recognized?"

"I knew Taff and his haversack well from our four years' joint service in the War."

"And where did you find this haversack you so conveniently recognized?"

"What do you mean?"

"This is not a question of word usage. This is a question of fact. It is simple. Where did you find the haversack?"

"In a room."

"What kind of a room?"

"A storeroom."

"A storeroom in which building?"

"Why, in the very building in which we now sit. The Olam Arms Hotel."

"On what floor in the Olam Arms Hotel?"

"The basement."

"Was this storeroom in the basement of the Olam Arms Hotel locked?"

"You bet," Goldwater said. "The lock was excellent and presented some difficulty, which I overcame."

"How did you overcome this excellent lock?"

"With a ballpeen hammer."

Abbey said to Cady, "Your Honor, Mr. Goldwater has just admitted that he acquired the alleged haversack and its alleged contents by breaking and entering a basement storeroom in this building, the very building in which this Courtroom is situated, not to mention where Your Honor maintains his current personal residence."

Cady was glaring at Goldwater.

Abbey went on. "Your Honor, if this common burglar can break and enter in one location, what is to prevent his taking his larcenous pilferage to every floor and every room of this building, including Your Honor's own private residence?"

Abbey turned to Goldwater. "Is there no end? Is anyone safe from your thievery?"

"Everyone is safe from me," Goldwater said, "Except those who steal and hide and lock up the precious personal inheritance left to me by deceased comrades and friends."

"Are you referring to this Court?" Abbey demanded.

Goldwater shrugged.

"Really," Abbey said. He turned to Judge Cady.

But the judge showed no interest. He told Abbey, "Please proceed."

Abbey stared at him. Did the judge's indifference perturb him? Maybe he was used to having his own way in Cady's courtroom.

Lamont had warned Goldwater to expect to lose, but things were going much better than Lamont had predicted. Something else was going on.

Abbey gave a small shake of his head and turned again to Goldwater. "You claim that his schematic you seek to introduce into evidence is an authentic original from John Taff?"

"Yes."

"Because you found it in this haversack you stole?"

"I found it in John Taff's haversack which I recognize from four years of constant companionship under the most intense travail."

"And you claim that this schematic is in his handwriting?"

A trick question. "Not really."

"Oh?" Abbey's right eyebrow rose hair-ward. "And why is that?"

"The schematic is nothing but lines and text. The text is printed by hand. There is no handwriting as such."

"Is the document notarized?"

"No."

"Witnessed?"

"No."

"Signed by John Taff?"

"No."

"Or anyone else?"

"No."

"So, If I may summarize, you lack any evidence to support your claim that John Taff wrote this schematic?"

"Not so."

Abbey stopped. He stared. Goldwater could guess what Abbey was thinking. Either he could ask what evidence Goldwater was talking about, or skip it, and let Lamont ask on redirect examination, which Lamont certainly would.

Abbey made his choice. "I shall bite, Mr. Goldwater. Please explain to the Court any flimsy evidence you can concoct that it was Taff who created that schematic."

"The language for one" Goldwater said. "All the text is in German. There are not that many German mining engineers in our town."

"But there could be some?"

"Could be," Goldwater admitted. "Though I have met none. Have you?"

Abbey ignored the question. "And you have been in this town fewer than two weeks?"

"True."

"You are not a mining engineer yourself?"

"I am not."

"You have not inspected the Bloody Angle mine yourself?"

"No."

"Even if you did inspect the mine, you would lack the expertise needed to confirm that the mine follows the schematic?"

"That much I admit."

Abbey shook his head. He said, "I have finished for now."

Lamont said, "Your Honor, we call Mr. Oliver Mack to the stand."

Goldwater stood and went to the door. When he opened it, he saw Olly standing out in the hall, clothed in the finery of a business suit. He said, "Olly, you are on."

Olly doffed his bowler and sauntered in. He took a spare chair. Cady swore him in and Lamont examined him.

It turned out Olly knew a lot about mining. He had mined for years, not only for silver, but gold and copper. He had also seen the Bloody Angle mine close up. He explained that the mine was "the safest I have seen in all my years," and went on to explain why. His testimony was thorough and detailed and peppered with arcane expressions like "adit," "base bullion," and "diluvium."

Goldwater understood almost nothing Olly said except for his guarantee that the mine was "the safest in Christendom."

Against Olly's encyclopedic knowledge, Abbey seemed helpless. It was clear he didn't know mining terminology any better than Goldwater. After Olly's testimony, he said only, "No questions."

Lamont said, "Your Honor, we have completed our case."

Olly stood and bowed to Cady and walked out the door.

Abbey said, "Your Honor, the Receivership calls one witness. Call Jack Roker." Abbey stood and went to the door and opened it.

Roker came through the door and took the same chair Olly had given up.

Had Roker and Olly crossed paths outside? Goldwater didn't know, but he supposed that the hallway outside a courtroom door was an inconvenient location for a fight, even in Olam, Arizona.

As Roker testified, he claimed expertise in mining like Olly's but with less credibility. He had witnessed what he called the Bloody Angle's poor design and construction. He had warned Taff many times, but Taff wouldn't listen. Taff cursed him. He quoted Taff as saying, "I won't take a Johnny Reb's word, especially when that Reb is an Irish son of a bitch like you."

Roker shook his head. "His intemperate verbiage was very disturbing to my peace of mind."

The verbiage was none the John Taff whom Goldwater knew would ever have used.

"Taff's words offended you?" Abbey asked him.

The real Roker snuck out. "Damn right. What gives that Teuton bastard the right to look down on my Frog ass? Nothing, I say."

As he spoke these words, Roker glared at Goldwater as if he were another Teuton bastard.

Abbey asked, “And you personally witnessed the cave-in?”

Lamont said, “Objection. Leading. Assumes facts not in evidence.”

Abbey leaned back in his chair and sighed. He spoke with exaggerated precision. “Did there come a time when something happened to John Taff?”

“Yes.”

“What?”

“A cave-in.”

“Did you see this cave-in?”

“I heard it before I saw it. I was inspecting a nearby mine. I heard a loud series of crashes. I rushed to help, but it was too late. I had warned him—”

Here Roker stopped to emit a small sob. He looked down and covered his face in both hands. His shoulders shook.

Everyone waited.

Roker looked up over his hands. Grief contorted his face. He shook his head. “It was too late. That good man was altogether crushed.”

He lifted his left hand and with his little finger wiped a single delicate tear from one eye.

Cady looked on, impassive. Abbey had somehow managed to paint a sympathetic expression onto his face. In the back, Lafitte was scribbling furiously in a notebook.

Lamont was rolling his eyes.

“Your turn,” Abbey said to him.

Lamont waited several moments before speaking. For the entire stretch, he fixed Roker with an expression full of venom.

Roker gazed back at Lamont with his own expression, one of innocence which might have convinced even Goldwater, except that Goldwater knew that Roker must have worn it most days of his life.

Lamont asked, “You claim John Taff's mine was poorly constructed and unsafe?”

“That's what I said.”

“Based on your knowledge as a miner?”

“Yes, and it was common knowledge anyway.”

“Your true occupation is not mining engineer, is it?

“I never said it was. I'm only talking the common sense of mining, the things what everyone knows. From practical experience. I have years of practical experience.”

“Or is it safer to say that your most relevant practical experience lies elsewhere?”

“I don't know what that is supposed to mean.”

“Isn't your most relevant practical experience as murderer for hire?”

“I resent that.”

“Your true name is not Jack Roker, is it?”

“That's the name on my saddle.”

“One previous name is in fact Jean-Baptiste Moliere?

“How did you come by that mistaken knowledge?”

“Common sense, as you call it. Plus, some who know you from elsewhere have recognized and identified you.”

“I'd like to know the bastard what said that lie.”

“So you can kill him?”

“I never told that.”

“Which leads naturally to my next question. Exactly how many men have you murdered under the name Jean-Baptiste Moliere?”

Abbey leapt in. “Your Honor, this question conflicts with Mr. Roker's rights under that palladium of our liberties, the United States Constitution, and specifically the Fifth

Amendment, which prevents self-incrimination. Lamont is asking the witness to incriminate himself."

"Likely true," Judge Cady nodded. "Objection sustained."

Lamont smirked. "Well then, Mr. Moliere, how about under your new *nom-de-meurtrier* Roker?"

Roker glared at Lamont. "What's that you just said?"

"It is French, Mr. Jean-Baptiste Moliere. Surely you understood. It means 'name for a murderer'. You were born in French-speaking Montreal, were you not?"

Roker shrugged. "What if I was?"

"Is Jean-Baptiste Moliere even your true original name?"

"Why shouldn't it be?"

"No particular reason." Lamont's smirk grew smirkier. "It's just that the actual Jean-Baptiste Moliere was the most famous writer in French, the French equivalent to our Shakespeare, a playwright who wrote under the name 'Moliere'.

"So?"

"It would be quite a coincidence to have two men separated by centuries and thousands of miles with identical names, would it not?"

Roker shrugged. "Oh, I don't know about that. You see, I am in the line of direct descent from that great man you speak of."

"You claim descent from a world-famous author?"

"Direct descent," Roker said.

"How the mighty have fallen," Lamont muttered.

"Objection, Your Honor!" Abbey said.

"Sustained," Cady said.

Lamont asked, "How did it come about that your mother named you after this author whose ancestry you claim?"

"My mother was a very literary person."

"A very literary person who did not know that the famous playwright's actual last name was not Moliere at all, but Poquelin?"

"Really?"

"Really."

"I wish someone had told my mother."

Lamont asked, "So what is your original name actually?"

Abbey said, "Same objection, Your Honor, Counsel is trying to bully Mr. Roker into incriminating himself. This is yet another violation of the Fifth Amendment."

Lamont asked, "How about it, Mr. Roker-Moliere-Poquelin? Is that correct? Just to tell the Court your earlier name would incriminate you in yet more crimes we as yet know not of?"

Roker grinned at Abbey. "I guess I'd rather not say."

Lamont slapped 'his thigh with a loud smack. "There you have it, Your Honor. Even this witness's supposed true name is fake. He is a Russian doll of fake identities, each identity hiding yet another killer inside it. For all we know, the man has ten names, each associated with its own set of monstrous crimes. In any case, I am finished with him for now."

He darted one last sneer at Roker, who showed no interest.

"I am finished as well," Abbey said.

"Well," Cady said. He nodded in an impressive display of thoughtfulness. "I have already ruled that everything is under advisement. I will let you gentlemen know."

"When?" Goldwater blurted, "Let us know when?"

Lamont elbowed him hard.

"Everything," Cady said. He glared at Goldwater. "Advisement applies to everything."

Cady smacked his gavelette on the plywood. "Court is dismissed. Everybody out."

Everybody but Cady stood and filed out. The last Goldwater saw of Cady, the man had gone back to staring into the corner again with that same morose expression.

Outside, Abbey and Roker and Lafitte trooped away down the hall and left Lamont and Goldwater standing together just outside the courtroom door.

"I don't get it," Goldwater said. "Why did Cady let us put everything into evidence? He seemed neutral, almost like a real judge. I did not expect that at all."

"I don't get it either," Lamont said.

"And then after everything, he takes everything under advisement. What does that mean?"

Lamont said, "It means he's waiting for some special event to tell him how to rule."

"What kind of event?"

"An excellent question."

A few more seconds answered Goldwater's excellent question. Doyle himself came sauntering down the hallway. He stopped to loom over the two men. He asked Goldwater, "Remember that offer I made you before, to forget this whole thing?"

"Of course," Goldwater said.

"I'm doubling that offer," Doyle said. "And I'll make sure you also get Taff's share of his claim. It's a great deal. You'll never do better this side of the graveyard."

Goldwater and Lamont exchanged glances.

"Now listen to me," Doyle said. "I know what it's like to dig the earth. I've hunted gold and silver and copper for years. The truth is, all the silver in Olam could not pay me back for my time and labor scouring these mountains for even a single speck of good ore. And I did it all alone and friendless."

He looked Goldwater in the face. “I know what it means to have no friend. Now I am offering to be your friend. Grab the offer while you can. Think about it.”

He turned and strode away.

“You see,” Lamont said. “We may have raised a few questions about the original determination that Taff died by accident, but we proved nothing affirmative about any murder. Yet here is Doyle offering you big money to drop the matter and go away. Do you see?”

“I do,” Goldwater said. “I see it very well.”

24 Blade Number 3: Misadventure in Olam

Olam *Blade*
Dateline: Olam, Arizona
February 19
From Editor Morris Goldwater

In his quest to obtain his fair share of John Taff's claim, this writer has once again set foot in the august courtroom of His Majesty Judge Arthur M. Cady. Since His Imperiousness has placed all matters under advisement, on this occasion we will refrain from immediate comment on any issue which arose in his courtroom today.

But we did learn more about other matters in Olam, and we write here to share our newfound knowledge with our fellow citizens.

For example, it appears that our fellow Olamite, known to us as "Jack Roker," is also a fellow of several other names. He picks up and discards his monikers with the disregard for comity which afflicts anyone who must race from place to place committing crimes as fast as he can, indeed with such speed and dexterity that he can never be pinned down to any specific place or name or crime.

The man is a miracle. Few possess the uncanny skill to operate in such a chameleon fashion. But then he is a special man, our Jack Roker, previously either "Moliere" or "Poquelin," and previous to those handles, who knows?

None among us in Olam, that much is sure. Unless it is Alexander Doyle, who, before employing Mr. Roker-Moliere-Poquelin-whatever, in the ordinary course of his business must have made some effort to ascertain his prospective employee's qualifications, previous experience and references.

This writer discovered these new facts about our Roker through the good offices of his attorney, Lawyer Lamont, in a Hearing before Judge Cady, while seeking to overturn Judge Cady's hasty earlier determination that John Taff died by misadventure, which for those not educated in the vagaries of legal terminology, is the law's way to say, "by accident."

It seems that "misadventure" means something related to but different from "adventure," which many account a good thing, although, like his cousin "mis," an "adventure" can turn out risky, as this writer can attest personally.

At the Hearing, Lawyer Lamont adduced substantial evidence suggesting that it was no misadventure which killed John Taff, but likely a garden variety murder, probably at the hands of Roker-Moliere-Poquelin himself, who admits to being the only witness and the last one to see John Taff alive.

Judge Cady promised to take all matters under advisement. For that reason, for now we will withhold description of many of the interesting events which befell at the Hearing.

But we will share two incidents of public interest which occurred after the Hearing.

First, immediately after the Hearing, Alexander Doyle tried to bribe this writer into dropping our case. To be fair, his offer was quite generous. We use this writing as a public opportunity to reject his graft with the indignation and contempt well deserved by all such attempts to suborn justice.

After all, we are not the only victims of his greed. We feel responsible not only to ourselves but to John Taff's inheritors and to every other Olamite whom Doyle has despoiled. To accept Doyle's shameful offer would have been to ratify a good man's murder and worse.

The second incident was that on this writer's way home, four assailants of unknown identity set upon him in broad daylight and battered him with knuckles and boot and club.

Fortunately, just when things might have "gone south," as they say, a noble friend and companion named Quinlan intervened and chastised the attackers and, with the aid of many indignant friends, sent the four assailants limping on their way.

Modesty requires us to confess that it was our friends who performed the majority of the thrashing while we lay helpless on the ground.

As Mr. Doyle did not yet know that we were going to reject his bribe, we interpret the attack as a warning, or at least as an encouragement to us to back off.

No doubt worse is yet to come. Whatever it will be, we and our friends stand ready.

25 Times Number 3: Yet More Goldwater Effusions, Hopefully Terminal

Olam *Times*
Dateline: Olam, Arizona
February 20
From Editor/Publisher/Reporter Oscar Lafitte

Morris Goldwater is not just a murderer but also a siren's wail alerting us to an intended reign of terror.

This fact is evident in every word he utters out loud or writes in the pretense toward journalism he calls his Olam *Blade.*

We have it on good authority, which we must credit, in that it comes from a source quite unimpeachable, that Goldwater swore in private, in his colorful way, to do Robespierre "even better," and set the heads of those who thwart his malignant designs "bouncing like bowling balls down the slime-infested streets of this backward burg."

Robespierre, as all students of history know, was the leader of the Jacobins, the revolutionary faction which turned France into a charnel house and abattoir during their revolution in the most recently completed century.

Goldwater and his gang now threaten a reign of terror worthy of those Jacobins, whose guillotines resounded with the thuds of fallen blades and the racket of bouncing heads.

Thousands died in that infamous Reign of Terror. Now Goldwater promises another one, not in the France of long ago and far away, but in the Olam of here and now.

Thus speaks the scoundrel who pretends to be a gentleman of integrity and respect.

We will name his Gang of Terror here. There is Goldwater himself, the leader and chief malefactor, followed by Victor Sadler, the failed businessmen whose resentments and jealousy have soured like bad wine into a vinegar rage toxic not only to himself but to the virtuous sister who must share his house, as well as the slaphappy drunk and ne'er-do-well Olly Mack, plus sundry assorted gang members, who lurk like virulent carriers, planning to spread their plague of anarchic violence to the entire town.

We will not permit their planned destruction of decent order to proceed.

When the time comes, we must meet steel with steel and lead with lead.

26 The Thumping

The morning after his thumping Goldwater lay in bed most of the morning, recovering.

The beating had been more brutal than he suggested with his flippant brief acknowledgement in the *Blade*. Every body part hurt. His left shoulder pained him most. An attacker had aimed a mighty blow with a truncheon at Goldwater's head but missed when Goldwater ducked.

After Goldwater stopped by Lamont's office to talk over Doyle's offer and the best way to reject it, he had been walking home down the Boardwalk. As he passed the Easy Money Saloon, he noticed four men loitering together just outside its door. They eyed him with obvious hostility and muttered some foul words, but he ignored them. The instant he passed them, one of them reached out and tipped his derby by its brim and flipped it off his head.

He didn't see which man did it. He turned around and looked them over. The four roughs were swiveling their heads about, looking at everything but him. The minor hat tipping seemed insufficient grounds to shoot them, even in Olam, though once again he considered it. Keeping both eyes on them, he bent over and felt around on the wood Boardwalk floor. He found and picked up his hat and set it on his head.

He turned to walk away. The biggest of the four reached out and tipped his hat again.

This time Goldwater saw who did it. Goldwater grabbed his hat out of the air with his left hand and took one quick step forward and punched the hat tipper in the chin with his right.

At first Hat Tipper looked surprised, but other than catching him off guard, the punch had little visible effect. Instead he swung a looping right of his own.

Goldwater ducked. The punch went wild over his head. He backed away. He faced the four and lifted his arms in front of him in the London Prize Ring boxing stance he had seen in the *Gazette*.

A mistake, it turned out, or at least pointless. The four roughs swarmed him, Hat Tipper leading the way. Goldwater dropped his stance as soon as they began raining punches on him. One of them brought a truncheon to bear and swung at Goldwater's head with it. Luckily he caught only Goldwater's left shoulder.

The blow was enough to knock Goldwater off his feet. Hat Tipper jumped down and began raining punches down at his head. Goldwater locked his arms above his face to fend off the punches. He felt painful kicks in his sides.

He had decided he was finished when a massive arm and hand came out of nowhere and lifted Hat Tipper in the air and threw him aside. The arm and hand were connected to Quinlan.

Olly Mack showed up too. In another instant at least a dozen miners were streaming out of the Saloon and into the melee.

The London Prize Fighting Rules went unobserved. The miners brought hammers and picks and employed them with enthusiasm. In an instant, three of the roughs had fled without Hat Tipper, who lay out cold in the mud street, now hatless himself and bleeding from his exposed crown.

Quinlan extended his giant hand down to Goldwater, who grabbed onto it and let Quinlan lift him and set him upright.

Whoops and cheers followed.

For the first time, Goldwater got to celebrate victory in a battle. Every victory in the War had come at great cost in comrades wounded and killed. After one of those, Goldwater never felt joyful, just exhausted and sorrowful and determined to do better next time.

This fight was different. No one was dead, at least no one who mattered, and injuries to everyone but maybe Hat Tipper were nothing but annoyances. What was a black eye or a sore shoulder to a man who risked his life every day by digging deep underground with the entire earth threatening at any moment to collapse on his head?

When Olly shouted for every man there to join him in Easy Money, Goldwater was glad to go along. A glass or two of whiskey would be just the thing.

Eight men gathered in front of the bar and drank themselves stupid. Goldwater had no money, so he had to let others buy for him, but they claimed to be glad at the chance, and he took them at their word.

Sometime in the next few hours, Quinlan came up to Goldwater and nudged him with his elbow. "I took care of the jocker who poisoned that kid like you asked."

Goldwater focused his eyes on Quinlan. He found it hard. Everything was blurry. "What?"

"You know, that hobo who burned Roland with acid," Quinlan said. "I took care of him."

Goldwater said, "I never asked you to do that."

"Sure." Quinlan winked. "Anyway, that's the last time he'll burn any kid with acid."

"I never asked," Goldwater said.

"Sure." Quinlan winked again.

"Well, okay, then," Goldwater said. He turned back to the bar for another drink.

The celebration lasted long into the night and deep into morning, and once more Goldwater found himself creeping up the back stairs to his room as quietly as he could manage.

He made it to his bed and was lying on his back trying to make the ceiling stop spinning when Marie opened his door and stood there.

She said, “I heard you,” and disappeared.

Sometime later, Marie brought a small white plate with two leftover hardtack crackers. She set the plate on the small table next to his bed. “This is your breakfast,” she said, “And your morning coffee.” She disappeared again.

When he woke up later on, his head and his banged-up left shoulder were fighting it out to see which could punish him more.

He got up long enough to take care of his ablutions. He poured a glass from the water pitcher to wash down the cakes he forced himself to chew and swallow.

He lay down in his bed and closed his eyes again.

27 Disaster

Goldwater was still lying on his back in his bed when gunshots woke him.

Maybe Roker wanted to emulate General George Washington, victorious Trenton one Christmas morning by surprising hungover Hessians still in their underwear.

Although, when Goldwater jumped out of bed, he was still wearing his glad rags from the day before, now rumpled and dirty and torn.

The gunshots multiplied. He ran to the window which overlooked the street. At least a dozen men were firing on the Sadler House, including Roker, who seemed to be leading the charge as they rushed the building. Roker ran too close to the building for Goldwater to shoot down at him.

But Goldwater spotted Hat Tipper across the street. He was easy to pick out. He was the one wearing the white rag around his head.

Goldwater fumbled his pistol out of his right-side coat pocket and took aim through the window and fired.

He thought he had hit the man, but Hat Tipper only grabbed his ribs as if a mosquito had stung him. Alerted to Goldwater's presence, he looked up at Goldwater and lifted a Winchester and fired several quick shots one after the other, pumping his lever each time.

Goldwater ducked away from the window. A few rounds came through it and smashed into the wall behind Goldwater. A few others penetrated through the wall facing the street. One struck Goldwater in his right shoulder.

Luckily, like Goldwater's own round when it hit Hat Tipper, this round only stung. The wall had slowed it from killing velocity.

Goldwater now had a wounded right shoulder to match his sore left shoulder.

Goldwater lacked firepower. At this distance, his .31 caliber pocket Colt could barely reach a man, and even when it did strike, the bullet only scratched and did not kill.

Goldwater was wishing for the Henry Repeating Rifle he had carried at Allatoona Pass, with its .44 caliber rounds.

He gave up on his upstairs window and raced down the front stairs. He reached the dining room just in time to see disaster.

Roker stood in a doorway. Roker must have broken through the front door. Victor stood facing him with a small revolver. Roker lifted his big Colt in his right hand. They both fired at once. The explosions shook the room.

Victor fell. His fall revealed Marie standing behind him. She had already leveled her shotgun. Like an avenging Fury, she fired a blast which tore through her brother's killer and seemed to double him over.

The blast deafened Goldwater. His ears rang for hours afterward.

She dropped her shotgun on the floor and ran forward to Victor and bent over him.

Another Doyle invader stood where Roker had stood, staring down at Roker, his rifle cradled useless in his arms. Goldwater sighted on him with his Colt and was about to fire when the man dropped his weapon and ran.

His flight left Goldwater with no one to shoot.

Hat Tipper stepped in. Goldwater lifted his pistol again to fire when another blast from behind cut Hat Tipper down. His fall revealed Olly Mack standing behind, his own shotgun smoking in his hands.

It was not the first time Goldwater stood feeling useless and futile after a battle.

28 A Lull

That afternoon, after the battle at the Sadler House, Goldwater, Olly Mack and Quinlan were sitting around Olly's regular table at the Easy Money, trying to figure out what to do next. Olly and Quinlan were nursing their whiskeys, but Goldwater was avoiding any booze for now; he was drinking a big glass of water to wash his parched throat. It was his fourth big glass of the afternoon. He could not quench his thirst.

"Doyle is holed up at the Olam Arms," Goldwater told the other two.

Olly Mack asked, "You know this how?"

"The boy Roland saw him go in," Goldwater said. "And has not seen him come out."

"You find that convincing?" Quinlan asked.

"I have instructed Roland to stay where he can see the Hotel back door," Goldwater said. "And he has pals watching the front. I trust them. Roland will tell me if Doyle comes out."

"You mean when, don't you?" Olly asked. "Eventually, he must emerge."

"I do not propose to wait," Goldwater said. "Even now he may have new hirelings on their way here as reinforcements, and I do not propose to dawdle until more enemies show up."

"Even so, more enemies will come," Olly Mack said.

"When they come, they must find Doyle dead," Goldwater said. "And finding no one to pay them, they will lose interest."

Quinlan asked, "How do you intend to make this death happen?"

"I will shoot him," Goldwater said.

Quinlan and Olly looked at each other. Goldwater stared at his nearly empty glass of water. Something living might be swimming around in those few remaining drops. But he saw nothing.

Finally Olly spoke, “To me that seems a trifle optimistic, Major.”

“The Olam Arms is three stories high,” Quinlan said. “Doyle could be anywhere in there, on any floor and in any room.”

“That is true,” Goldwater said.

“Doyle can simply lie in wait for anyone who comes,” Olly said.

“That is the reason he has chosen that building to hide in,” Quinlan added.

“And an excellent reason it is,” Olly added.

“That is also true,” Goldwater said. “But I have my own advantage. Thanks to Doyle’s fool who dropped it and ran, I will be handling my favorite weapon. The best rifle I have ever used. Unlike my pocket Colt, the Henry is a true weapon of war.”

“The Henry Rifle?” Olly asked. “The one Colonel Mosby called that damned Yankee rifle that can be loaded on Sunday and fired all week?”

“The very one,” Goldwater said. “During the War, I bought one with my own money. I hoped it would save my life.”

Quinlan said, “Crazy Horse used the Henry to help him wipe out Custer. All Custer’s men had were single-shot Springfield carbines and a few Colts.”

Goldwater said nothing. He had his own opinion of Custer and the man’s reckless charges. Custer’s mindless daring had helped the Union win at Gettysburg but had left him and his men high and dry at Little Big Horn.

“Didn’t you yourself describe Doyle as the quickest gun in the Dakota Territory?” Olly asked.

"The so-called quick draw is a mere bagatelle," Goldwater said.

"That does not square with my experience," Quinlan said.

"A man's speed on the draw will prove even more pointless against a rifle than against a pistol," Goldwater said. "What matters is the accuracy a man derives from his steadiness of nerve. John Taff told me that. Then he showed me how to act on it."

"I got hold of a Henry one time during the War," Olly said.

"How did you come by it?" Quinlan asked him.

"A dead bluecoat I ran across," Olly said. "The man had no further use for his. But I never got to fire it once. We had no ammunition to fit the thing. Eventually I chucked it as so much dead weight."

Goldwater smiled a grim smile. "I will not have that problem. I checked the load. Along with the rifle, Doyle's coward gifted me with sixteen rounds still in the magazine."

"That may do it," Olly admitted.

Goldwater said, "If sixteen rounds will not suffice, I should just give up now."

"That is the first thing you have said which makes sense," Olly agreed.

"Yes," Quinlan said. "You should give up right now, before entering into this dangerous enterprise, in which you will be Chicagoed for sure."

"We know you are righteously angry about your friend Victor Sadler," Olly said. "But what good is revenge?"

"Oh, I don't know about that," Quinlan said. "Revenge can be damned sweet, is my experience."

"Revenge has nothing to do with it," Goldwater said.

"You going to take Doyle on alone?" Quinlan asked. "There's no need. We can put together a bunch to take out Doyle."

"I have seen too many die in these idiotic mass frontal attacks," Goldwater said. "Thousands. Tens of thousands, in fact, ordered into pointless death by idiot generals who all imagined themselves to be Napoleons."

"That much is true," Olly Mack said. "I have seen it too."

Goldwater said, "What many cannot accomplish in a frontal attack, one man can do alone by stealth. And I have a way in."

Olly nodded. "You mean the back entrance?"

"I do," Goldwater said. "I will sneak in through the back door the way I snuck in to recover John Taff's haversack. Then I will move upstairs and search floor by floor and room by room until I find Doyle."

"And then Doyle will shoot you," Quinlan said.

29 A Dustup

Quinlan and Olly managed to convince Goldwater to wait for dark before heading to the Olam Arms.

Goldwater used his free few hours to revisit the Sadler House. To get in, he had to step over pieces of a shattered front door. Doyle's assassins had smashed apart the dining room table at which Victor and Marie had sustained him. The killers had broken its legs to pieces and perforated its top with at least a dozen bullet holes.

Someone had taken the bodies away. Goldwater hoped it was kindly souls who had done it.

No one greeted Goldwater. He climbed the stairs from the dining room alone. On the second floor, Marie had shut her door against the world, including him. He stepped close to the door and held his ear near it. Inside, Charlotte was crying. Marie said something to her. Goldwater could not make out what. He did not knock.

He climbed the short flight of stairs to his own third floor room and went in. He opened his haversack and changed into his best suit. Might as well dress well for his funeral.

He filled and puffed on his briar and contemplated his life so far and waited for night. When darkness showed outside his window, he slipped down the back stairs and exited through the back door. He made his way across the rough ground behind the Boardwalk buildings to the Hotel. He carried his new Henry rifle. Out of habit, he carried his peashooter Colt in his coat's right pocket.

The moon was near full. On the way, he saw Roland standing as lookout behind the Easy Money. Goldwater stopped. "We haven't seen him come out of the Hotel," Roland said of Doyle.

Goldwater walked on, to the dirt yard behind the Hotel. Olly Mack sat cross-legged on the ground in the brush about twenty-five yards behind. Goldwater asked, "Did you bring your whistle?"

Olly shook his head. "Got no use for it, boss,"

Goldwater made for the servant's entrance in back. He spotted a blob in the shape of a man in the darkness nearby and raised his Henry. Oscar Lafitte stepped into the moonlight.

Lafitte smiled the same affable smile at Goldwater he had smiled every time before. He held his notebook and pencil ready down by his hip, poised to report.

Goldwater lowered his rifle. He caught himself gripping it tighter. If Lafitte knew Goldwater was coming, Doyle knew it too. So much for the element of surprise.

As Goldwater reached out with his left hand to pull open the back door, Lafitte winked at him. One more time since his arrival in Olam, Goldwater suppressed his impulse to shoot a man.

Goldwater tugged the heavy door open and went in and shut it gently behind him.

Once again all was dark.

He stood with his Henry cradled in his arms and waited to give his eyes time to use any smattering of light. To light a candle or even a match was to risk getting shot dead.

After a few moments, his eyes adjusted as well as he could hope. He could just make out walls on both sides of him and, below, a dark path forward.

He lifted his Henry in front of him to ready it for whatever he might run into. He took a single step forward and waited. Nothing happened.

Deliberating a while before each step, he took three more. On the third, his right elbow bumped against the wall.

Stupid. His Henry had no safety. This very moment its hammer was resting up against the back of a live cartridge. Even a slight impact on the rifle could fire off the chambered round and announce Goldwater to the entire Hotel, including Doyle.

Goldwater could reduce the risk of accidental fire by opening the lever wide, but he might need to fire in an instant. He kept the lever tucked close under the receiver.

Should he cock it or not? He could keep the weapon uncocked or he could thumb the hammer back and risk firing it after the mildest brush against the wall or anything else he bumped into in this Stygian darkness.

He thumbed back the hammer. If Doyle truly were the quickest draw in Dakota Territory, Goldwater would have to be ready to fire just as quick.

He should have noticed a way upstairs the first time he had snuck in this way, but he did not recall any stairway. He had been preoccupied with searching for the storeroom.

This time he spotted it in the gloom on his left, an unlit stairway perpendicular to this hallway. The stairs led upward.

He climbed the stairs one slow and steady step at a time.

At the first floor, he stopped. He stood at the junction of several short hallways. Gas lamps posted head high on the walls lit all of them.

Down one hallway was the main lobby. Although anything was possible, it seemed unlikely Doyle would hide out on the main floor. After all, this was a hotel, open for business. Too many strangers came and went for Doyle to feel safe on this level.

Goldwater climbed up the next flight. He reached the landing on the second floor. Doyle would be here or on the third and highest level.

The gas lamps lit the entire hallway, including six doors, three on each side. Goldwater should have no trouble seeing his way forward. He took a deep breath and set off down the hall.

Now his earlier brag seemed foolish, that he would throw open door after door. Any room might be holding a guest, and any guest would be primed to shoot any stranger stupid enough to surprise him by banging through his door. Goldwater was here to shoot it out with Doyle, not some innocent, well-armed lodger.

"Doyle!" Goldwater yelled down the empty hallway. ""The barnyard of which you spoke has emptied! One of your Yankee sheep has shown up. He has brought something for you."

Goldwater's shout echoed down the hall of closed doors. No answer.

"Doyle, you cur! Come out and present your traitor's face to a Yankee soldier. We have seen enough of your rebel backs."

A man stepped out of one of the doors. Goldwater leveled his Henry at the man, who was not Doyle, and who saw Goldwater and ducked back into his room.

Goldwater walked forward down the hall. Shouting did not work. Goldwater replaced it with a quiet voice which ought to draw out Doyle if anything could. He chose a string of insufferable insults which he dribbled into the air one at a time like pennies into a fountain: "Traitor. Grass-bellied, redneck, bottom feeding son of a bitch." And so on.

Goldwater walked down the hall, adding new personal insults one after the other, changing only his choice of words. After one trip up and back, always facing down the hallway, he stopped and uttered a single hard slur: "Liar!"

In this part of the world, "liar" was the worst insult Goldwater could think up. A known liar could not survive out here. Out here, any man who did not tell the truth at all times would be dismissed from other men's company. He would isolate himself forever. If the time came when he needed help, no other would show up.

Maybe that explained Doyle's momentary isolation and vulnerability.

Surprising himself with his mounting rage, egging himself on as went, Goldwater shouted the single word "Liar," over and over.

All his dormant and condensed anger bubbled out in that one word, a war cry he had never uttered, even in war.

He caught himself and stopped.

Still no response.

Try the third floor.

He climbed the steps to the third floor with the same caution as before.

No gas lamp was lit. The hallway up here was black as the basement down below.

Doyle's doing, no doubt.

He raised his Henry and aimed it into total darkness.

At the other end of the darkness, a man-shaped shadow seemed to grow. Goldwater shifted his aim into the heart of the darkness and inserted his index finger inside the trigger guard and up against the trigger.

"No need to shout," the shadow said.

He was no more than fifteen yards away.

"I wanted you to hear me," Goldwater said.

"Every man in Arizona Territory hears you."

"I wanted that too," Goldwater said.

Doyle fired fast, too many times to count. Before Goldwater could pull the trigger on his Henry, it exploded in his arms. The butt struck Goldwater's ribs and knocked him backwards.

He found himself lying on his back on a soft carpet. Excruciating pain lanced his ribs with every breath he gasped in or out. His hands shook in uncontrollable tremor. It took him a moment to realize that Doyle's bullet had struck the rifle stock. Goldwater's Henry had spared his life, at least for the moment.

Goldwater had not even seen the man draw. Doyle came quick as advertised.

Goldwater dropped the pieces of his broken rifle. He placed shaking hands down on the carpet and began to push himself to his feet. He stood on trembling legs and reached into his coat pocket to grab his pistol.

Doyle still planted himself in the same spot. He had re-holstered his gun. He wore the grin of a man who enjoyed doing what he was good at. What he seemed good at was the quick draw Goldwater had heard about.

Doyle took two steps toward Goldwater, closing the distance. He drew and fired, once again too fast for Goldwater to see. Goldwater's right ear burned. No rifle shielded him now. He lifted his pocket Colt and took careful aim at Doyle's midsection, the biggest part of the big man's big body, a target he could not miss.

Doyle watched Goldwater's deliberate movements with amusement. He smirked the same smirk he wore that first night in the barn. He drew and fired once more. Goldwater thought he heard the round whiz by his left ear.

Goldwater fired once, then several more times. Goldwater's first small round found Doyle, but not in the midsection where Goldwater had aimed. A small dark hole popped into existence in Doyle's left cheek. For an instant, Doyle stood stiff. The hole leaked red. Doyle's right hand slackened. The revolver in it drooped loose and fell to the carpet. Doyle followed his pistol and toppled face forward.

"A lucky shot," Goldwater claimed afterwards, and he was telling the truth, more or less.

30 United States Marshall Hiram Davis

As great Caesar's fall transformed Rome, Doyle's fall transformed Olam, except that what followed was not civil discord and war, but peace, at least until the next petty tyrant took over.

A new Territorial Judge stepped off the inbound train. He was a large man who carried with him a large suitcase, which contained a man-sized gavel and a sheaf of warrants, along with a document bearing the signature of the President of the United States, who designated him the new Judge for Arizona Territory.

The Silver Ring was broken.

Judge Cady left town just in time. To where, few knew. Any who did know said nothing. Goldwater wondered if the judge had taken along with him some of his advisements.

Besides Olam's new Federal Judge, another newcomer was a United States Marshall.

Goldwater was standing behind the counter in Victor Sadler's store when the newcomer showed up. Goldwater had stepped in to handle Victor's business until Marie could sort things out. Now that Doyle was gone and the competition he created was also gone, business at Sadler's was picking up.

Every move Goldwater made stabbed him with new pain, in both his shoulders and in his bandaged ribs, which, thank God, were not broken, just badly dented.

Because Olam lacked any doctor, it had fallen to Marie to wrap the bandage, a task she performed with strength and skill. It was nothing; she had nursed mangled men before. This was another of her deeds for which he was grateful, although at the time, he felt a self-conscious embarrassment at her touch, an embarrassment she ignored.

In his store and his books, Victor had left behind only disorder. Goldwater could not even identify the stock. He had commandeered Roland to work at the shelves and help him inventory. A good job for a kid. Roland was doing that job now, sorting through some small boxes and bottles on one of the shelves at the side of the store.

The Marshall strode through the front door like a general into a camp. Goldwater recognized him right away. He wore the same long dark coat and boots he had worn the previous time Goldwater had seen him more than twenty years previous. It must be a sturdy coat. Or maybe he had bought an identical replacement.

The man was Deputy Marshall Hiram Davis. The previous time Goldwater had seen Davis, back long before the War, he had come to Ojibwa City searching for a slave catcher named Murphy. Murphy had disappeared from the world without a trace. What made the disappearance a federal matter was the fact that Murphy operated under the authority of the Fugitive Slave Act, which of course was now defunct, or as lawyer Abbey or Lamont might put it, "moot," thanks to the War and the subsequent 13th Amendment banning slavery forever.

Davis recognized Goldwater too. "Damn," he said. "Mr. Goldwater. You do show up at the most troublous times."

"As do you," Goldwater said.

"That is my employment," Davis said. "I go where trouble happens. What is your excuse?"

"I have none," Goldwater said.

Davis grinned. "I mean, other than your apparent natural inclination to foment trouble."

"Which brings up the natural question," Goldwater said, "Did you ever find Murphy?"

Although of course Goldwater knew the answer. Murphy was unfindable, at least by mortal man.

"Never did," Davis said. "Not even his remains. But I guess it don't matter no more, what with slavery being altogether outlawed now."

"Slavery is indeed outlawed," Goldwater said. "Though it was a hard enough thing to make happen."

"I suppose you fought for the Blue?" Davis asked.

"Yes."

"As did I," Davis said.

Goldwater took a moment to enjoy a fleeting bond with this man who was no doubt willing to shoot him down without any shilly-shally. "You have an iron memory for recognizing me," Goldwater said. "And I much admire good memory in a man."

"Thank you," Davis said. "I admire you too, if only for your iron determination to avoid saying anything useful to me, in which course I anticipate you will persist this time, as you did on the last occasion when we met."

From the first, Goldwater had spotted a change in Davis he could not get a fix on. Now he saw it. He said, 'I see by your badge that you are no longer a mere Deputy. You are now a full-fledged United States Marshall. I congratulate you on your promotion, Marshall Davis."

"Thank you," Davis said. "Believe me, I earned it."

"I do believe you," Goldwater said.

Roland had stopped his work at the shelves. He was holding a small box of liver pills. He stared at Davis. Davis glanced at Roland and smiled. Roland did what he did, which was to stare back.

Goldwater filled the silence. "Marshall Davis, is there anything else I can do for you?"

"You have not done nothing for me never." Davis said. "And I suppose that on this occasion you will not change your custom not one whit." Davis turned and walked out of the store.

So much for the law.

Goldwater turned and said, "Roland. Time for lunch, boy."

"Yes, sir," Roland said. He set the box of liver pills down on the shelf and walked over to the counter.

Goldwater reached around and took the black metal lunch bucket off the shelf behind him and set it on the counter. He said, "Let us see what splendid repast Marie has provided us." He opened the lid.

"Sandwiches," Goldwater said. "Excellent."

As if Marie ever made them anything else.

"What kind?" Roland asked.

"Once again, we have both beef and chicken," Goldwater said. He waved toward the open lunch bucket. "You may choose."

Roland peered into the lunch pail. He said, "Will it be all right if I take the chicken?"

"I said, 'You may choose', didn't I?"

"I know. You did say that."

"I did."

Roland reached out his right hand and held it over the open pail. He glanced up at Goldwater. Goldwater smiled a paternal smile down on him. Roland grabbed the sandwich as if filching it off a widow's windowsill. He said, "I'll just take this one here on top."

"That is fine," Goldwater said. "I will be very satisfied with the other."

Roland took a bite of his sandwich. He swallowed. His glance flickered over to another shelf at the side of the store.

"Go ahead," Goldwater said. "Grab yourself one of those soda bottles."

"Which one?" Roland asked.

"Any one you want. And get one for me too, please."

Roland walked over to a shelf and took two bottles, both strawberry red. He carried them over to the counter and watched with patience as Goldwater pried off the caps with his Barlow.

Through it all, Roland's expression remained somber. Roland was so solemn in everything he did, even the pursuits a nine-year-old boy should find fun.

For a while, the two ate and drank without speaking, until Roland asked. "Mr. Goldwater, will you be leaving Olam soon?"

"Yes."

"Going home?"

"Yes."

"To be with your wife and children?"

"Yes."

"To take care of them." More a statement than a question.

"That is my duty," Goldwater replied. "As well as my pleasure."

"What will I do here?" Roland asked. "In the meantime?"

"What do you mean?"

"Just that," Roland said. He stared directly into Goldwater's eyes. "Can I come with you?"

The question stunned. To take a child from his natural family while any of its number survived? Unheard of. Goldwater had not even imagined such a question being put to him. He asked, "What about Marie?"

"What about her?"

"She would miss you," Goldwater said. "She loves you."

"No, she doesn't," Roland said. "She loves Charlotte. She sees in me only a burden."

Silence followed. Roland chewed on his sandwich and nipped small swallows from his soda bottle and stared up at

Goldwater, watching without expression as Goldwater interrogated himself with one tough question after another.

How had Roland come to see Goldwater this strange way? A substitute father, was that it? For a boy who had no man in his life? Was it some particular thing Goldwater had done? He had made no special effort toward Roland beyond the natural kindness he would show toward any child he happened to meet.

Could his Ojibwa City home hold another boy, especially one as wild and unpredictable as Roland? Was there even room?

Finally Goldwater said, “I will have to think over this thing. And I will have to ask Marie.”

“You will see,” Roland said. “She will be glad to get shuck of me.”

31 Lost Vigor

Standing in the open doorway, Marie said, "I see you have found Victor's hoard."

It was past midnight. Goldwater was sitting on the big rug, sorting through Victor's personal items. Marie had started the project of cleaning them out, but after the first few minutes, she fled in tears. To spare her more pain, Goldwater had volunteered to clean out Victor's room. Of course, he promised to identify and save any Sadler family items for her.

He was going through a trove of Victor's books and magazines. Marie showed up just as he was examining an incriminating pink page of the latest Police *Gazette*.

"This is not the way it looks," Goldwater said, relying on the time-honored phrase men have employed to explain the inexplicable to women.

She smiled a sad smile. "Allow me to guess the section. 'Footlight Favorites'?"

"Your guess is a correct one."

She took two steps into the room. "That wretched rag was one of my brother's treasures," she said. "Believe it or not, he even subscribed. He could not wait for it to show up in Mel's Barbershop or in the Easy Money so he could snatch up a copy and fetch it back to his room. He especially liked the actresses. I think he favored the buxom ones in the skimpy garb."

"Many men do," Goldwater said.

She asked. "Have you run across his treatments?"

"Treatments?"

"For lost vigor," she said. "I understand that advancing age can give rise to lost vigor in men. He seemed very concerned about this condition. He was always in pursuit of a solution. He bought many products."

Goldwater knew the products she meant. He stocked a few at his Emporium. They included assorted useless pills and ointments. The device requiring a dry cell battery was one he had declined to stock.

"I have found no products of the sort you mean," Goldwater said. "But how did you become aware of this supposed lost vigor of his? Men do not often share such information with their sisters."

"The matter is simple enough," she said. "He brought home packages he refused to open in my presence. Sometimes he sneaked them up the same back stairs you employ after your own nighttime wanderings."

"If he hid the packages, how do you know what was in them?"

"Why else would he hide them?"

Goldwater defended Victor. "You assume much."

She shrugged. The shrug drew Goldwater's attention to the female body under her clothing. Her nightgown was scarcely more than a shift, of some thin fabric unlike her usual sturdy calico. For the first time in his presence, she wore no corset. She was also barefoot. Her feet were pale, almost translucent. They seemed too small for her and somehow out of character with her general sturdiness. He could see her cotton chemise and pantalets through an opening in the side of her gown, which draped over her in a fashion all too disturbing.

Her shrug animated a powerful feeling in him. Perhaps it was the shape of her strong shoulders or the swell of the breasts under her chemise.

He managed to ask, "What do you know of these men's matters?"

"I am a widow," she said, "My husband is dead, but I am not dead myself. I have been married. I have a daughter. The ways of men are not a total mystery to me. Yet there are many things I do not understand about men."

"Which things?"

Her directness surprised him. "Why the whores? You must know about them, in the shacks by the railroad tracks. Victor made use of them all the time."

"How do you know that?"

She shrugged again, putting his feelings in greater turmoil.

"I do not know all the reasons men visit whores," he said.

"I was hoping you could explain," she said. "I certainly do not accept the contention of some women, that all men are but animals."

"Nor do I," he said. "Victor was not an animal."

"Surely not," she agreed with a sad smile. "But you cannot explain these ways of men?"

"I cannot." Although he could come pretty close, he thought, as he looked at her.

She asked, "Do you?"

"Do I what?"

She sighed. "Visit whores, of course."

"I do not," he said.

There was no legitimate reason for the condescending expression she assumed to sting him, but it did. He suppressed the impulse to tell her that his vigor was getting along just fine but was also something he saved for his Rosalie.

She must have guessed yet again what he was thinking. She nodded as if he had answered the question she had not asked. She said, "Hence the six children. But there must be moments, of loneliness, of longing, of questions."

"There are," he admitted. "Moments, I mean."

For a moment one of those questions hung in the room between them.

Having no answer he could permit himself or impose upon her, Goldwater sat and waited.

She waited too, perhaps for one moment too many. Then she turned and walked out of the room. Her scent stayed behind, hanging in the air, a fragrance of lost opportunity.

Goldwater knew two things.

The first was that his vigor was in no way lost.

The other was that he would never again come across Marie without her corset.

32 A Cruel Relinquishing

"Rosalie!" he called.

Goldwater untied his cravat and let it drop one more time. The two blue-and-white-striped strands hung down on his chest, further evidence of his fumble-fingeredness, as if he needed any.

"Rosalie!" he called again. No answer. Where was she?

He wanted to dress himself in complete finery for his stroll over to the Ojibwa City Bank to deposit the first money order from the Bloody Angle.

Olly Mack had mailed the money order. Goldwater was going to insist that Olly transfer the next payment via Western Union. Western Union was the up-to-date method for sending money across country, and by far the safest, as it avoided the risk from banditry and the vagaries of post office operations.

Just now, Roland was off at a local vacant lot playing the ball game with his new brothers. He was a butterfingered baseballist, and in that respect, a true chip off the old block, nothing like Goldwater's natural sons and the Wilder boy, not to mention the Dropo scalawags who roamed Ojibwa City making nothing but trouble.

Ever the dutiful husband, Goldwater had telegraphed Rosalie from Olam to get her assent to his bringing Roland home with him.

Her reply telegram was typical Rosalie: "What unhousebroken puppy will you be bringing into our home this time STOP I should never let you out of my sight STOP. But I know you will do what you want regardless STOP And one more mouth cannot starve us so feel free and go ahead and please only yourself as you always do STOP"

A typically wordy and unnecessarily expensive Rosalie telegram, with her standard excess and expensive verbiage. After all, Western Union charged by the word after the first ten.

But it was just the way of her.

He knew ahead of time she was going to love the urchin at sight, which was exactly what happened. If Goldwater knew nothing else, at least he knew his wife.

Goldwater lifted the two ends of his ascot up near his throat for another try.

A try at a tie. Kind of amusing. Maybe he should set pen to paper again. He could craft that phrase into something longer and submit what he wrote to Noble Shandling over at the Ojibwa City *Savage.*

Now that Goldwater had developed his small skill at writing English language prose for publication, it seemed a waste not to indulge it back home. Perhaps he could begin a new career as an author.

Since coming home, his only new writings had been the German-language letters he sent across the ocean trying to locate any wife and children of John Taff. No response so far in any language.

His new try at a knot failed. The two strands drooped down on his chest again. Where was Rosalie?

Of course, he had not dared cross the wilderness with a nine-year-old boy the same hobo way he had always traveled before. His first cash advance from the Bloody Angle in hand, Goldwater had steeled himself and forced himself to pay sound money for two railway tickets, the first railway tickets he had ever purchased in his life.

Handing the coins across the counter felt like a cruel concession, as if he were relinquishing along with the pieces of metal an essential portion of his life, his misadventurous youth, a phase he had clung to in recent years, expending on that futile effort all the grim resolution he had once spent hanging barehanded onto the icy iron rods under a boxcar.

Rods or youth, hanging on for dear life could take a man only so far.

Next, he might find himself sitting atop a horse. At the mental image, he shuddered. Then he laughed.

He must share this laugh. She would understand.

He called again, “Rosalie!”

THE END

Made in the USA
Coppell, TX
21 January 2026